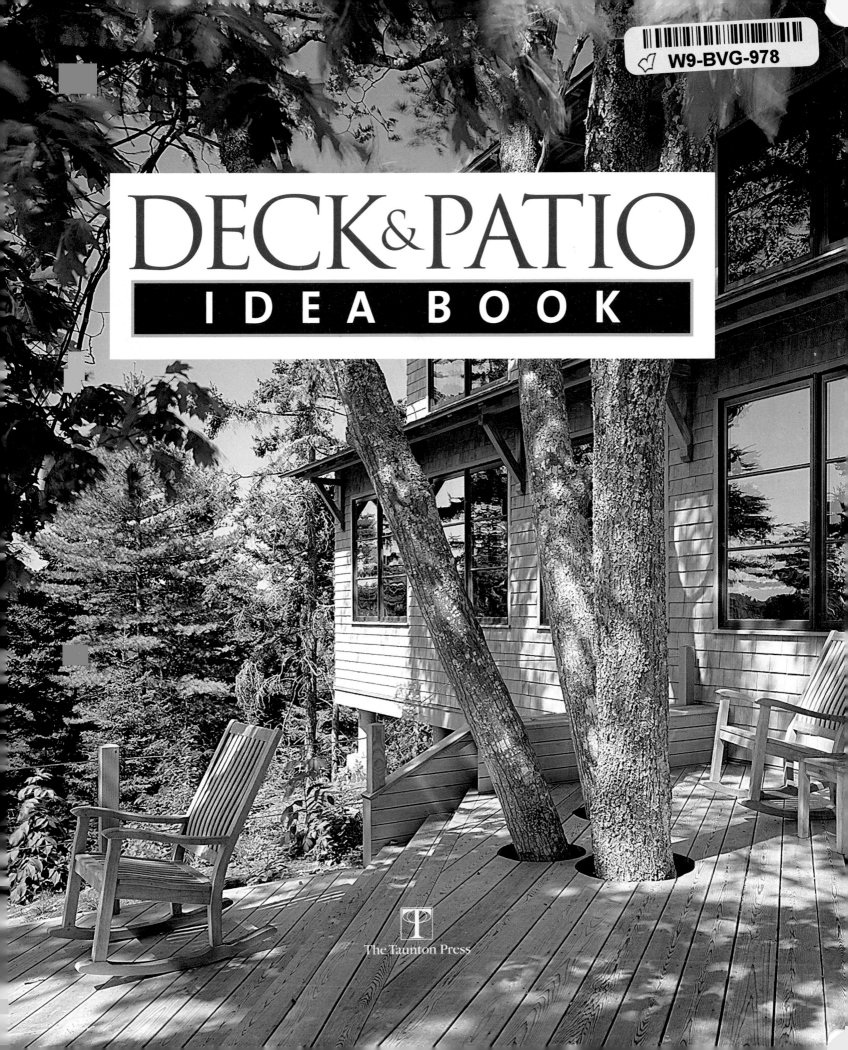

DECK&PATIO
IDEA BOOK

The Taunton Press

The Taunton Press
Inspiration for hands-on living®

The Taunton Press, Inc., 63 South Main Street, PO Box 5506, Newtown, CT 06470-5506
e-mail: tp@taunton.com

Distributed by Publishers Group West

EDITOR: Stefanie Ramp
JACKET DESIGN: Jeannet Leendertse
INTERIOR DESIGN: Lori Wendin
LAYOUT: Cathy Cassidy
ILLUSTRATOR: Christine Erikson
COVER PHOTOGRAPHERS: Front cover: top row left to right: © Brian Vanden Brink, Photographer 2003; Charles Miller, courtesy *Fine Homebuilding,* © The Taunton Press, Inc.; Andy Engel, courtesy *Fine Homebuilding,* © The Taunton Press, Inc.; middle row left to right: Charles Miller, courtesy *Fine Homebuilding,* © The Taunton Press, Inc.; © Robert Perron, Photographer; Charles Bickford, courtesy *Fine Homebuilding,* © The Taunton Press, Inc.; bottom row left to right: © Brian Vanden Brink, Photographer 2003; © Brian Vanden Brink, Photographer 2003; © Brian Vanden Brink, Photographer 2003; back cover clockwise from top left: © Brian Vanden Brink, Photographer 2003; Photo © Jessie Walker; © davidduncanlivingston.com; © Brian Vanden Brink, Photographer 2003

Library of Congress Cataloging-in-Publication Data

Stillman, Julie.
  Taunton's deck & patio idea book / Julie Stillman.
     p. cm.
  ISBN 1-56158-639-0
  1. Patios--Amateurs' manuals. 2. Decks--Amateurs' manuals. I. Title:
Deck and patio idea book. II. Title.
  TH4970 .S74 2003
  728'.93--dc21

                              2003012630

Printed in the United States of America
10 9 8 7 6 5 4 3 2 1

The following manufacturers/names appearing in *Taunton's Deck & Patio Idea Book* are trademarks:
Trex ®, Brock Deck®, Nexwood™

Acknowledgments

This *Idea Book* is a result of the efforts of a creative team—editors, authors, photographers, illustrators—whose geographic locations spanned several states and who endured ill-timed computer meltdowns, bitter cold and raging snow storms, and a few personal crises while working on this book. This acknowledges that effort and offers a pat on the back and handshakes all around.

Contents

Introduction

We all crave that special place to relax outside—some open-air territory to retreat to after spending the day in a hermetically sealed workplace. Whether looking for a small spot to sunbathe or read in solitude, or some slightly more elaborate space to have breakfast, entertain, or stargaze, an outdoor room provides gracious living space outside. And as part of our culture's current focus on a healthier, happier lifestyle and making our homes our castles, building a deck or patio expands the footprint of the house—embracing the outdoors and enhancing both our property and our well-being.

Decks and patios add another dimension to the home, giving you the freedom to enjoy the outdoors in comfort without leaving your backyard. And since you are literally building from the ground up, the design of outside "rooms" is not constrained by walls or quirky dimensions.

You have a blank canvas waiting to take the form of whatever you fancy—perhaps with some allowances made for budget and zoning laws.

No longer just bland squares of pressure-treated lumber nailed to the backs of houses, decks have taken on new shapes, surfaces, and levels. And patios have evolved from an indifferent slab of poured concrete to encompass a wide range of forms and materials— from the warmth of brick to the sophistication of bluestone to the casual appeal of gravel.

In this book you'll find hundreds of ideas to inspire you to move beyond the "wouldn't it be nice" stage and really start

parts of the home, you'll also see the range of amenities that are now common, such as spas, gazebos, and outdoor fireplaces. In addition to the photos, the book includes numerous illustrations detailing deck and patio components, as well as sidebars on topics of special interest.

Taunton's *Deck & Patio Idea Book* offers a multitude of useful and inspiring ideas and design solutions for your deck or patio. We hope this book, along with your creative ingenuity, will assist you in building a beautiful outdoor room that provides relaxation and comfort for years to come.

designing your outdoor room. We begin with a planning primer on how to evaluate your site and examine various approaches to design. The core of the book is a photographic exploration of the varied decks and patios that can be built and the features that define them, including railings, built-ins, and overhead structures.

Hundreds of photos depict the full spectrum of styles and sizes, from the simple wraparound deck to the curved, multilevel redwood deck with an outdoor kitchen; from the small brick patio to an elaborate series of terraced patios with stone walls. And because decks and patios have developed into outdoor rooms that are equipped and furnished like other

Great Deck and Patio Designs

Optimizing your outdoor living spaces increases your home's usable square footage and lets you create and maintain a connection to nature. These restorative outdoor retreats possess the best of both worlds—the comforts of home combined with the sights, smells, and sounds of your natural surroundings.

Ideally, the outdoor "rooms" for a house are designed concurrently with its construction, ensuring a seamless flow in design that blends indoor and outdoor living spaces into one great property. However, with good planning and attention to detail, a deck or patio can be added at any time and still look like an integrated part of the home and landscape, rather than something tacked on or artificially grafted. Along with thoughtful design, let your imagination guide you to create the outdoor room of your dreams, adapting your wish list to fit the reality of your needs, your budget, and your site.

Making these outdoor rooms as inviting and comfortable as your indoor rooms is a worthwhile endeavor—you can spend just as much time on a well-designed and nicely appointed deck or patio as you do in the family room, but with the added benefits of fresh air and a lovely view.

◀ ANGLED OFF THE FACE OF THE HOUSE to capture the best views, this unaffected yet well-conceived deck was shaped to form a protected corner for the table and chairs, while leaving a clear walking path from the back door to the steps and pathway. Built-in benches provide casual seating and good protection from an accidental step-off.

▲ THIS OUTDOOR ROOM could just as easily have been a porch, but the owners opted to leave the deck open to the sun and added a pergola instead. The pergola, latticed fence, and pool combine to lend a transparent feel—in counterpoint to the solidity of the house.

CHOOSING A DECK OR PATIO

In planning your outdoor living spaces, one of the first considerations is whether you want a deck or a patio—or both. Although decks and patios come in all forms, decks tend to feel more like extensions of houses, whereas patios seem more integrated with the landscape because they sit directly on the ground. While the site will occasionally make the decision for you, you often can incorporate either with careful planning.

Patios are more versatile in terms of design and budget because of the broader range of materials that can be used, and unless a patio is cliffside, it won't require rail-

ings as a deck would, affording even more freedom in design. Patios can also tolerate a lot more water (from rain, snow, and pools) than wooden decks, and so require less maintenance.

Building codes should be taken into account: Decks are considered structure under building codes, requiring building permits and review by inspectors; typical, ground-hugging patios are landscape elements, requiring no construction permits. Both decks and patios must meet local zoning codes as far as setbacks and coverage, however, so always do your research before you start to build.

Interlocking Forms

TOO OFTEN A RECTANGULAR DECK or patio is thoughtlessly tacked on to the back of a rectangular-shaped house, yielding a three-sided playpen of no distinction. A better-designed arrangement is when the shape of the deck or patio forms an interlocking relationship with the shape of the house, fitting the two together like puzzle pieces. This marries the indoor and outdoor spaces. The deck or patio should then in turn interlock with the landscape, allowing the same puzzle-piece connection with the yard and plantings.

▲ BOTH AESTHETICS AND FUNCTION ARE SERVED by this second-floor deck that was conceived of as part of the house, not just tacked on later. The deck's height permits a shaded patio area below.

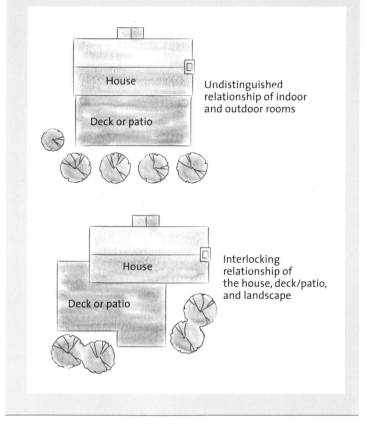

House

Deck or patio

Undistinguished relationship of indoor and outdoor rooms

House

Deck or patio

Interlocking relationship of the house, deck/patio, and landscape

Other factors to weigh before deciding on a deck or patio are the style of your house, topography, views, ease of delivering building materials, and, of course, the cost of materials and labor. All of these factors will vary greatly from site to site, from region to region, and according to design.

Deck Details

Traditionally, decks have been built of wooden planks laid on a wooden framework that's supported by posts on a firm foundation. Today, however, synthetic materials—such as synthetic wood planking and PVC railing systems—offer alternatives to natural wood, though they can't be used for the structural components.

A deck has to be thoroughly designed before construction begins. The structure of the deck must be engineered so that it meets

Anatomy of a Deck

A DECK IS COMPOSED OF **four major components** that together function as a single system, ensuring a secure and sturdy deck: foundation, framing, decking, and railing. The foundation ties the deck to the ground. Holes are dug down to a depth below the frost line and filled with concrete. The framing is a combination of vertical wood posts connected to the concrete foundation and horizontal framing (joists) that spans the distance between the wood posts and the house. The decking is the finish floor of the deck, and the railing is the protective surround.

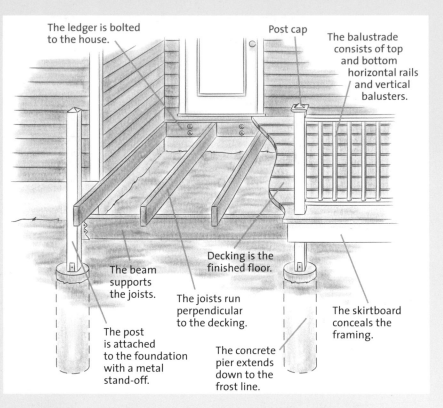

The ledger is bolted to the house.

Post cap

The balustrade consists of top and bottom horizontal rails and vertical balusters.

The beam supports the joists.

Decking is the finished floor.

The post is attached to the foundation with a metal stand-off.

The joists run perpendicular to the decking.

The concrete pier extends down to the frost line.

The skirtboard conceals the framing.

▲ IT'S UNUSUAL TO SITUATE A DECK AT THE FRONT of a house, but because this site faces a Florida beach, the large deck alongside a screened porch becomes an entry courtyard, connected via French doors to the entry, great room, and formal living and dining areas.

all the requirements spelled out in the building code and crafted using the best construction practices and methods. This doesn't mean that you have to hire an engineer, but you should follow the requirements as far as joist spacing and railing heights and rely on an experienced carpenter to build a securely fastened railing that won't fail.

Patio Primer

Patios are fashioned from either stone, tile, concrete, or brick units set directly on the ground in a sand base or adhered to a concrete slab with mortar to create a more permanent, solid, and level patio. For a more casual space, patios can also be formed using loose gravel, rock, or pebbles contained by a solid edge, such as brick.

Because a patio is more a landscape element than a part of a house, its design can be less rigid than a deck's and can deviate more from the house's architectural style. A patio can take on a free-form look, for instance, with uncut fieldstones laid in a random pattern, or it can be a polished, orderly surface. Site, space, budget, and personal style will all influence the kind of patio you choose to build.

As with decks, there are practical considerations, too. Patios are affected by temperature changes. As the ground freezes and thaws, it moves and so will the paving if it is not laid on a sand or gravel bed that will permit the groundwater to move without disturbing the patio. Make sure that you enlist the help of a skilled mason (or educate yourself on paving mechanics) during design and construction.

▲ THIS TYPE OF RAISED STONE PATIO is uncommon, more an architectural extension of the house than part of the yard. The large, square stones set in a gridlike pattern express some of the same crisp lines as the overhanging roof.

Anatomy of a Patio

THERE ARE TWO BASIC TYPES of patios: patios where stones sit on the ground and patios where stones sit on a concrete base. A cross section reveals the difference between the two.

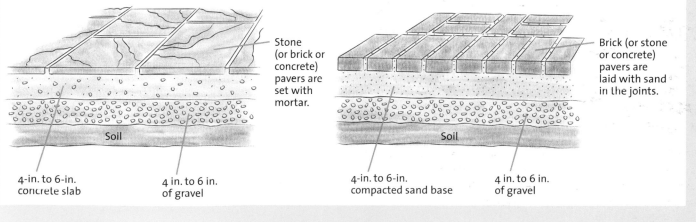

PATIO SET ON A CONCRETE SLAB

Stone (or brick or concrete) pavers are set with mortar.

Soil

4-in. to 6-in. concrete slab

4 in. to 6 in. of gravel

PATIO SET ON A SAND AND GRAVEL BASE

Brick (or stone or concrete) pavers are laid with sand in the joints.

Soil

4-in. to 6-in. compacted sand base

4 in. to 6 in. of gravel

▲ AT THIS SITE, THERE WAS A CLEAR CHOICE of where to situate the patio for the best view, the sun and shade, and the privacy. Even when you're inside, just a glimpse is all you need to know that there is a pleasant spot beckoning just out the door.

DESIGNING OUTDOOR ROOMS

Whether you choose to build a deck, a patio, or a combination of the two, there are several considerations that apply to both. First, you have to determine where the outdoor space should be located. There's no simple location formula; it is a complex design challenge that requires you to thoughtfully evaluate your property in terms of the landscape and orientation of the house, as well as establish your wants and needs in terms of budget, shape, material, and size of the deck or patio.

It's important to integrate your deck or patio with the house and the yard for a variety of reasons: aesthetics, enjoyment of your property, safety, and resale. To accomplish this, there are a number of issues to address when planning a deck or patio, such as site evaluation, climate, usage, and budget.

Site Evaluation

The natural shape of the land—your yard's dimensions and the extent of any slope—as well as the shape and location of your house on the property will affect the design of your deck or patio. A steep slope may warrant a terraced deck or patio, whereas a narrow lot might determine a longer overall shape for your outdoor rooms. An L-shaped house will gracefully accept an L-shaped deck or patio, while a

◀ ▼THE OWNERS OF THIS HOUSE WERE DETERMINED to create an outdoor room to enjoy the dramatic view downriver. The rocky riverbank makes it hard to send posts down, so the deck is held by chains suspending it from the house, and it is also braced.

strictly rectangular footprint might benefit from a wraparound deck that helps root it in the land.

It's a good idea to obtain a site plan or plot plan, which you can get from a surveyor or the town, or it may be a part of your deed documentation. This document will reveal the legal parameters for locating any new structures or coverage. Setbacks that restrict building on certain portions of your lot or limitations to additional paving will certainly affect your planning.

You can also make a "balance sheet" for your site, itemizing the assets and less desirable features of the yard. Ideally, the deck or patio will take advantage of and enhance all the good features, while compensating for,

PLOT PLAN

A typical suburban lot tends to be deeper than it is wide, with the house placed midway along its length. The available area for a deck or patio is bounded by the house, as well as the front, side, and rear setback lines of the property.

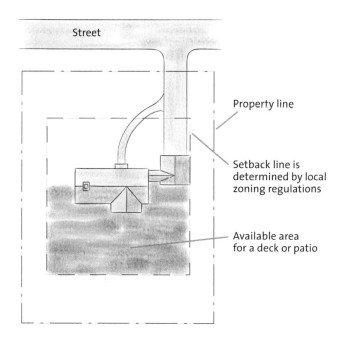

Property line

Setback line is determined by local zoning regulations

Available area for a deck or patio

and even concealing, the bad. Think in terms of a sunny spot—with some natural shade, if at all possible—that faces an appealing view, provides some privacy from the street and neighbors, and is easily accessed from the house. For many homes, this is best accomplished in the backyard, but if it happens to be on the side of your house, there's nothing stopping you from locating your outdoor room there.

Climate

The primary goal of any outdoor space is to help you enjoy being outside. When planning a deck or patio, this means making the most of sun and shade and taking into account prevailing winds, especially if you are building near water or on a mountainside.

▲ON THIS NARROW LOT, PRIVACY WAS A PARAMOUNT CONCERN that was accommodated by using a decorative privacy fence at the upper deck. The brick patio is screened by plenty of plantings.

SHAPING AN OUTDOOR ROOM TO THE HOUSE

If you are adding a deck or patio to an existing house, the shape of the house often suggests the complementary arrangement for attached outdoor rooms. The interior arrangement of rooms will also influence the orientation of the deck or patio, as will the position of the sun, the views, and other site features.

Rectangular

L shaped

U shaped

Four-square

Courtyard

The relationship of your house with the site, and also with the sun, will guide you in locating an outdoor living space. Generally, in the northern part of the country with shorter summers, a southern-facing deck or patio is preferred as long as it can be shaded for part of the day. In the southern part of the country where summers are brutally hot, an outdoor room is best located on the shadier northern or eastern sides of the house. A western orientation can be difficult, since the setting sun tends to be glaring and very hot in all regions. But a spectacular western view may win out, yielding a patio or deck with extra shading devices or additional plantings to compensate.

Pay attention to the types of trees that are nearby: Coniferous trees that hold their needles year-round make good windbreaks but will provide shade in the spring and autumn when you want more sun. If you properly position a deck or patio adjacent to deciduous trees (which lose their leaves in the

Outdoor Lighting

PLAN FOR ANY LIGHTING during the design phase of a deck so that you can integrate the wiring and fixtures into the construction. Don't try to simulate typical indoor light levels—the point is to be outside at night, and it should feel like it. You can always supplement permanent lighting with tabletop lanterns, candles, and moonlight. Lighting for the outside consists of primary lights that shine brightly to illuminate outdoor spaces and secondary lights that create a mood, delineate a built feature, or highlight a natural feature.

Primary light examples:
- A wall-mounted sconce by a doorway or a garden wall
- A pole-mounted fixture along a pathway
- Floodlights for pool parties
- Motion-detector lights for security

Secondary light examples:
- Lanterns strung along a wire for outdoor dining
- Lights that shine on stair treads
- Strings of small lights (like Christmas lights) wound through trees or shrubs
- Landscape lighting tucked among plantings to cast a glow

▲ ON A TIGHT SITE, THE ROOFTOP may be the only option for locating a deck with the best views, sun, and privacy. The slatted chaises match the weathered clapboards, tying in the décor with the architecture.

▲ THIS GLOWING ORB casts just enough light to illuminate the outer edge of the deck. There is also a wall-mounted sconce on the house, and between the two locations, there is ample nighttime illumination.

SUN AND SHADE THROUGH THE SEASONS

During different seasons, the sun's angle changes. Use this to your advantage when planning decks and patios.

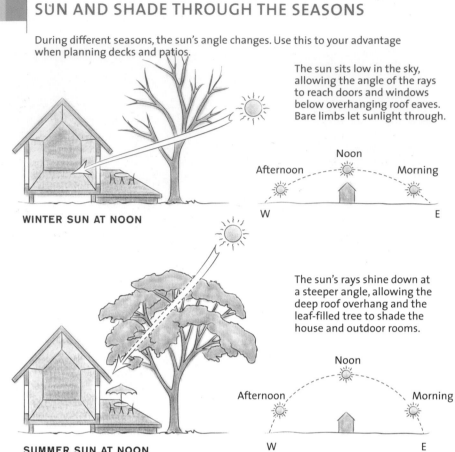

The sun sits low in the sky, allowing the angle of the rays to reach doors and windows below overhanging roof eaves. Bare limbs let sunlight through.

WINTER SUN AT NOON

Afternoon — Noon — Morning
W — E

The sun's rays shine down at a steeper angle, allowing the deep roof overhang and the leaf-filled tree to shade the house and outdoor rooms.

SUMMER SUN AT NOON

Afternoon — Noon — Morning
W — E

▲ **A PERGOLA GIVES NEEDED SHADE** from the midday sun on this rooftop patio of slate pavers. The purlins (horizontal members used in roof construction) run perpendicular to the overhead joists, adding another layer of shade-casting material.

winter), you can take advantage of their shade in the summer and direct sun in the cooler months.

Drainage is another important consideration: Both decks and patios should be designed with a slight slope away from the house to direct the rain off onto the ground where it can percolate back into the soil.

Use and Access

Another important part of planning your deck or patio is examining how you envision using your outdoor room. You'll soon realize you want a space that fulfills many of the same functions as the indoor rooms: a place to cook, a place to gather and eat, a place to play, a place to nap, and some storage space.

▲ A SHELTERED COURTYARD IS good for a windy site, and the indoor and outdoor spaces here are knit together to form a yin-yang exchange. The patio area is used primarily for dining and entertaining, and the second-floor deck is for sunbathers.

SPACE FOR FURNISHINGS

As with an indoor room, it's important to plan for furnishings to ensure that each has enough room to be used comfortably.

8 ft.

8 ft.

TABLE FOR FOUR

12 ft. to 14 ft.

8 ft.

Benches and picnic table

TABLE FOR SIX OR EIGHT

3 ft.

3 ft.

4 ft.

Maintain clearance from flammable fences and railings.

Locate grills at least 10 ft. from any building to guard against fire hazards.

GAS OR CHARCOAL GRILL

48 in. to 60 in.

20 in. to 30 in.

TWO-SEATER BENCH WITH BACK

72 in. to 84 in.

30 in.

CHAISE LOUNGE

Landscaping

LANDSCAPING ELEMENTS should be designed along with a deck or patio to ensure a complementary flow between the two. Start with what you already have, be it trees, rock outcroppings, good views, or water—an existing natural feature of the landscape can be the focal point for any outdoor room, whether it is a distant view of mountains, a nearby stand of birches, or a backyard rock garden. Then add to the overall effect by incorporating planters and establishing places for greenery that are integrated into the design of the deck or patio. Well-designed landscaping will underscore a site's best features. A gardener or other landscaping professional can suggest plantings suited to your purpose and climate.

▶ A DECK OR PATIO should not be arbitrarily plopped down onto the ground, but rather, it should tie the house to the landscape. By gracefully interlocking built and natural forms, this house feels like a natural extension of the surrounding landscape.

You also need to plan what the circulation paths will be to, from, and within your deck or patio. For convenience, a large patio off a family room should be accessed easily from the kitchen, but a small deck off a master bedroom is a private retreat and does not need to be part of any circulation path. Plan in advance where furnishings and appliances will go: Where will the chaise lounge get the best view? Where will the table be convenient to the kitchen door? Where is the safest, most convenient place for the grill?

Position the stairs and accessways onto the patio or deck so that there is a clear path to any door into the house without having to navigate around tables or chairs. The design of the deck or patio should guide the circulation path so that the different use areas are not bisected by circulation routes.

Budget

As with any other major expense, it's important to establish a budget for your deck or patio project. And just as with building a house, you'll have to weigh the factors of building big versus building better. You may have to grapple with decisions such as whether to build a large, rectangular deck with less expensive materials, or a smaller deck with levels or interesting architectural features built of a higher-grade wood. Or you may have to decide between an understated patio built of found fieldstones set in a sand base versus an elegant bluestone terrace set on a concrete slab with a surrounding stone wall.

For a deck, your budget might be almost equally split between labor and materials; for patios, much of the cost is for the labor, though concrete and natural stone are cheap compared with cut bluestone or fancier granite paving materials. Both decks and patios can be easily tackled by an experienced do-it-yourselfer, so you'll save a lot if you can provide your own labor.

Working with Professionals

IT IS A LITTLE INTIMIDATING to know how to begin to make your ideal patio or deck a reality. Knowing who to hire and what they can do for you is key.

■ **A surveyor** prepares the plot plan or survey, which is like a scale map of your property that locates the legal property lines, your house and other buildings, and any other major features of the site, such as driveways, rock outcroppings, paths, and trees.

■ **An architect** is a licensed professional with years of training who can design a deck or patio and prepare the detailed drawings from which it will be built.

■ **A landscape architect** is a licensed professional with years of training who can design the total landscape. This includes selecting plant materials and preparing detailed drawings from which the deck or patio will be built.

■ **A builder or contractor** is the person who actually constructs the deck or patio for you from a set of drawings that he or she might produce, or from the more detailed drawings that the architect or landscape architect may have prepared.

■ **A mason** is a contractor who is skilled at constructing things from stone and concrete. This is the person who can build a stone wall, patio, or steps from drawings that someone else prepares, or from a drawing that he or she might produce.

■ **A carpenter** is a contractor who is skilled at constructing things from wood. There are contractors who specialize in building decks and who can also supply you with design services.

◄ THE INNOVATIVE ZIGZAG EDGE of this alluring patio allows the plants to encroach and knits the patio into the landscape. The patio follows the slope of the gentle hill through flowers and greenery.

Decks

ECKS ARE RELATIVELY NEW ARRIVALS to residential architecture; prior to the 1930s houses had either porches or patios for the purpose of outdoor relaxation and entertainment. Simply defined, decks are room-shaped floors without walls or ceilings— a man-made landscape, generally located on the back or most private side of a house, which extends its footprint.

Decks can hug the ground or float like treehouses, and range from simple rectangular platforms to multilevel structures with complex architectural details. When planning a deck, it's important to integrate it into the landscape while complementing the house, so shape, materials, and plantings should be considered carefully.

And a deck should receive the same thoughtful outfitting as an indoor room; depending on the atmosphere you wish to achieve, it can simply house a couple of deck chairs (what else!), or it can be a full-blown room with all the amenities.

◄WHEN THE OWNERS OF THIS LARGE HOME did a major renovation in the Craftsman style, decks and stonework were added, creating both visual interest and useful outdoor space. By making the lower corner posts larger than those in the balustrade, a visual hierarchy and pleasing sense of rhythm are established, which also break up the mass of the house behind.

Deck Types

WHETHER YOU DESIRE A PRIVATE DECK off an upper-level bedroom, a wraparound party deck with a view of the ocean, or a children's play deck off the family room, certain considerations must inform your planning. The shape and style of your home and the size and orientation of your property will be the primary determinants when deciding on the type of deck you build, and a well-designed deck takes advantage of what a home already has to offer.

Although decks come in all shapes, sizes, and levels, there are five basic categories: platform decks, raised decks, second-story decks, multi-level decks, and freestanding decks (see the illustration on p. 24). Angular, geometric shapes are easiest to build, but curved decks are possible, though they must be planned carefully and are more costly.

▼ BUILDING CURVES INTO A DECK takes more time and labor, and thus costs more, but the results can be spectacular, as witnessed by this multi-level redwood deck. The decking is 2x6 redwood boards, and the serpentine railing is made up of thin strips that can be bent easily.

▲ THIS RAISED DECK CAPITALIZES on a stunning panoramic view, and the horizontal cables in the railing cleverly echo the horizon line without blocking it. Sturdy deck materials and furnishings were selected for this seaside meadow site to withstand the winter squalls.

◄ AMBIENT LIGHT from the house's large windows spills out onto this simple platform deck with chairs perfectly positioned to watch the sun set over the water. That might be all you want for exterior lights, especially in a natural setting like this one where a lack of pollution allows the stars to be a twinkling centerpiece at night.

▲DESIGNED FOR ENTERTAINING, this angular free-standing deck has a multitude of components: a sunken spa, outdoor kitchen, lattice fence, and built-in benches and planters. Redwood is a good choice for a large deck that is a whole play area because of its natural durability.

►THE ROUNDED EDGE OF THIS ALLURING DECK is repeated in the cascading steps that lead down to the lawn, lending it an unusual shape reminiscent of a small man-made hillock tucked up against the house. Ringing a deck with steps lets you forgo the use of a continuous guardrail around it, allowing an uninterrupted view.

◄▼ THIS COMMODIOUS AND CURVY DECK made of ipe seems to set sail into the landscape, offering a much more interesting silhouette than a straight deck would. The underside of the deck is hidden from view by a continuous wooden skirt that conceals the deck's structure, hiding the posts and joists within the graceful curve. The sinuous railing—with a balustrade of wrought-iron panels between rhythmic posts—accentuates the shape of the deck.

DECK TYPES

Any deck is a unique construction, custom designed and built for a particular house and to meet particular needs of the homeowners. The basic types of decks shown here are general categories to help in planning the type of deck that suits location and usage.

PLATFORM DECKS
Low to the ground; no need for railings or steps; can take any shape.

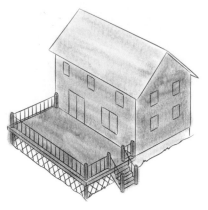

RAISED DECKS
Raised a few steps above the ground; require protective railings and steps to grade.

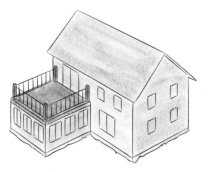

ROOFTOP DECKS
Set on top of a flat-roofed portion of the house; require careful installation to maintain waterproof roofing.

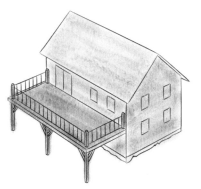

SECOND-STORY DECKS
A deck that's a full story above the ground; may or may not have stairs to the yard.

POOLSIDE DECKS
Extend around inground or above-ground pools; may incorporate a building code-required fence.

WRAPAROUND DECKS
Any deck that takes a turn around a corner of the house.

CREATING A COUNTERPOINT to the rounded wall of the house, this platform deck takes the straight tack, with a bump-out at the apex of the curve for visual drama and a seating area. The narrow section of the deck outside the curved windows is left free from embellishments that would block the view from inside.

▲ THIS EMBRACING, WRAPAROUND DECK blurs the distinctions between front, side, and back, creating for the house a sense of fluid location in the landscape while taking advantage of the multiple views. Making the deck entrance a natural continuation of the grassy path leading to it further enhances the deck's organic feel.

▲FANCIFUL FAT COLUMNS stand sentry at this deck that's built low to the ground in the crook of a house with many nautical references (the owner wanted to mimic a tugboat). The belly of the column is repeated in the shapes of the house and the outward-swelling balusters on the second-floor deck.

▶DESIGNED IN CONCERT with the house, rather than tacked on as an afterthought, this unusually shaped deck is the result of a limited site and the desire to capture as much daylight and passive solar radiation as possible. The curve of the south-facing deck hugs the house, making it an extension of the living space inside.

◄ AROUND THE CORNER from the triangular decks, the sawtooth edge of the house is juxtaposed to this straight shot of deck. The planking is laid on the long direction, accentuating the length of the deck and forming mini-rooms within the crooks of the building.

◄ THIS HOUSE BOASTS TWO UPPER-STORY triangular decks that jut out into the air like arrowheads, embracing the landscape and view. To maintain unobstructed views from the lower-level family rooms, each deck is designed to be supported by one main post.

► LAYING DECK PLANKING on the diagonal is a dynamic alternative to orienting the planking parallel or perpendicular to the house. Here, the resulting sawtooth edge of this raised deck creates interesting nooks to house seats or plantings.

DECKING PATTERNS

The direction and pattern that the decking takes starts with the layout of the supporting framing. The simplest pattern is to lay decking at 90 degrees to the framing, making sure that seams between the ends of the planks fall over framing below. Diagonal decking patterns, curved edges, and basketweave patterns require more framing beneath.

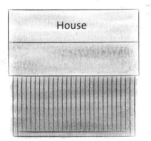

Perpendicular to the house

Parallel to the house

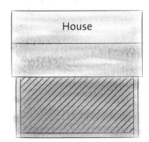

Diagonal

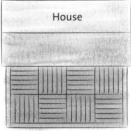

Parquet or basketweave

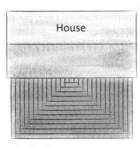

Herringbone

Sectional

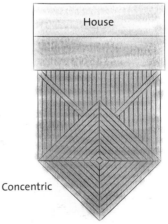

Concentric

◄▲ THIS SPACIOUS, RAISED DECK is perfect for entertaining, with its multiple lengths converging in the circular seating and eating area, which is further distinguished from the rest of the deck with an eye-catching, concentric decking pattern. The vertical skirting mimics the siding on the house, creating natural flow between the structures.

▲HAVING DECKS ON DIFFERENT LEVELS allows for a variety of outdoor activities. This rooftop deck, which recalls a widow's walk in old sea captain homes, lets you sunbathe in privacy; the second-floor deck is a quiet retreat off the bedroom; and the main deck is perfect for beachfront entertaining.

◀ THIS SECOND-FLOOR SEATING AREA and deck bridge connect to a covered porch for all-weather access to the outdoors. With stellar views of Puget Sound to be had, the railing was designed with a double top rail to minimize visual interruption from the balusters.

▲ A TOWER-TOP DECK under its own pitched roof is a shady destination that frames the views of the valley. Building a deck on a roof requires careful planning, however; the underlying roof has to be flat and waterproof (see the sidebar on p. 32).

◀ THE UNDERSTATED, COZY BALCONY off the bedroom is just large enough for a pair to take in the spectacular sunset. The rustic planking and railing and simple chairs blend well with the woodsy surroundings.

Decking Over a Flat Roof

B UILDING A DECK on top of a flat roof requires care to avoid making holes in the roofing. Generally, a waterproof membrane is laid over plywood that is placed on top of the existing gravel or asphalt roof. Duckboards (small sections of prefabricated deck) are laid on top of the membrane, relying on gravity to hold them in place. For more secure rooftop decks, a ledger (a joist mounted against the side of the house to support one side of a deck) is attached to the face of the house with perpendicular sleepers (wood planks laid horizontally at wide intervals) aligned with the roof rafters below. The sleepers can be tapered to compensate for any slight slope in the roof to create a flat deck.

◄ THIS UNIQUE DECK exemplifies the many safety details that must be considered with a rooftop structure. A metal railing encircles the skylight, but a creative use of shape and materials makes it a centerpiece rather than a design oddity. The substantial height of the deck allows for beautiful views of the bay but also necessitates a sturdy—in this case, solid—railing.

◄ A MULTILEVEL DECK offers privacy and shade below and a view and sun up top; although the decks have separate accesses, a staircase connects them for maximum ease and utility. Upper-level decks require drainage considerations, and in this well-designed deck, rainwater flows between the planks onto the underlying roof, which is gently pitched to capture the runoff in the gutter system.

▲ SHORT PLANKS CAN BE REPLACED easily if they show signs of rot, especially in a pool/hot tub area like this where there will be lots of water splashed on the deck.

▲ REDWOOD MAKES A BEAUTIFUL, durable, and stable material for this contemporary multilevel deck with brushed stainless steel rails. To preserve redwood decking, a protective finish that contains mildewcides, water repellents, and ultraviolet protection should be applied every few years.

▶ THIS MAHOGANY DECK is built within a concrete wall that forms a substantial edge under the deck. The vibrant painted coping (covering) at the deck's edge acts as a visual transition between the natural wood and boisterous metal railing, which lends a casual playfulness to the structure. Narrow spaces between the decking planks accommodate wood's tendency to expand in warm weather and obscure uneven shrinking as the deck ages.

Choosing Deck Materials

A VARIETY OF DECKING MATERIALS are available, from domestic wood species to tropical hardwoods to synthetics and vinyl products. Price, availability, quality, and environmental concerns will affect your selection. Getting samples of the ones you're considering will help make your choice easier.

■ **Pressure-treated wood** is the least expensive, and one of the most popular, options. It's usually made of fir, southern pine, or hemlock (or some combination of hemlock and fir). Pressure-treated woods have a greenish-brown hue but can be stained if you find that unappealing. Be aware that the chemicals that make it rot-resistant include a type of arsenic. (This type of treatment is being phased out of use.) Although pressure-treated wood is safe to touch and doesn't leach into the ground, wear safety goggles and gloves if you are working with it, and never burn it.

■ **Softwoods** like cedar and redwood are beautiful and naturally rot- and decay-resistant, but they're more expensive than treated wood. Cedar is available in two species—western red cedar and Alaska cedar. Western red is reddish-brown and lighter and softer than Alaska yellow cedar or redwood. Yellow cedar has a clear, pale yellowish color, which weathers to silver-gray. Redwood, renowned for its rich hue, is very easy to work with and holds finish well.

■ **Tropical hardwoods,** such as mahogany, ipe, and meranti, are a luxurious option and extremely durable and resistant to rot and insect damage. However, they're expensive and can be difficult to work with.

■ **Synthetic wood planking** is an environmentally conscientious alternative to real wood and is splinter-free. However, synthetics are too weak to be used as structural framing and are used only for decking. Unlike wood, which requires a protective sealer every year, synthetics need virtually no maintenance but are more expensive. Synthetics come in several forms: Composite materials, such as Trex®, are made of recycled plastics and wood fibers, and vinyl decking is made from PVC.

▲A SAMPLE OF DECKING MATERIALS (from left to right): treated southern pine, redwood, Brock Deck® vinyl decking, pressure-treated fir, Trex® plastic composite decking, Nexwood™ plastic composite, ipe, Dream Deck vinyl decking.

▲ TREX® IS A POPULAR SYNTHETIC COMPOSITE decking and railing material made of recycled plastic and wood fibers. Splinter-free and moisture-resistant, it comes in several colors, and because it curves more easily than wood, it can be a good material to use for building curved decks and railings such as this one.

► PREMIUM DECKING MATERIALS, such as the redwood shown here, can take on a furniture-like appearance when well cared for, and the decorative wood accents inserted into the decking pattern enhance that effect. A concealed fastening system was used, which keeps the decking unmarred by nail heads.

◀ WOOD DECKING BY A POOL has to be carefully selected, as it must withstand a continuous parade of wet feet and chlorine splashes. This cedar decking has weathered to a silvery gray thanks to the effects of sun and water.

Deck Maintenance

PROPERLY FINISHING AND MAINTAINING a deck surface will prevent staining and rot and will keep it structurally sound and looking good for a long time.

Some wood species, like cedar and redwood, have natural water- and rot-resistant properties and can be left unfinished to turn a lovely silver over time. Most other woods must be finished with either a clear or semitransparent stain. These finishes will repel water, and some contain preservatives: fungicides, mildewcides, and insecticides. Pigmented stains and finishes also act as sunscreens and will help the wood retain its color.

Finishes must be reapplied every year or two to maintain the deck surface. Sweep, wash, and bleach if necessary between finish treatments, allowing the deck to dry thoroughly before applying the first coat of the finish.

Railings, Stairs, and Built-Ins

I N TERMS OF FUNCTIONALITY, safety, and aesthetics, railings and stairs are critical components of a deck and should be carefully designed. Both have detailed building code requirements, which vary by location and which will affect design, but with all the options now available, there's plenty of room for creativity. Railings can be made of a range of materials, from the traditional wood and metal to the more innovative glass and even mesh or netting. Stairs can take a variety of forms and be made from a number of materials as well to create interest while acting as a transitional element between deck and landscape. Built-in seating, planters, and storage are functional features that, when artfully constructed, can add some architectural spark to a deck. If substantial enough, they can also do double duty as railings.

▼ LIKE A WHITE PICKET FENCE, this fresh white railing helps create the sense of a garden room. While railing components like these fancy finials add substantial style to a deck, they can be easily purchased at a lumberyard or home center and are relatively inexpensive.

▲BUILT-IN PLANTERS AND BENCHES furnish this outdoor room under an open-air ceiling. As an extension of the living room, this deck mimics the layout inside with a planter serving as the outdoor alternative to a corner table flanked by wooden "sofas."

◄VARIOUS CONSIDERATIONS, from drainage concerns to capitalizing on a good view, may mandate that a deck be elevated, like this dramatic wraparound. While building codes govern all stairs and railings, they tend to be more specific when applied to elevated structures; for instance, codes restrict the amount of steps in a single run, so rather than a continuous descent on this stair, an intermediate landing has been incorporated.

▲ LYRICAL LIMBS FILL IN THE BALUSTRADE of this railing, and the shapes between the branches create unusually framed views of the trees and water. Peeled branches should be sanded to avoid splinters and sealed to maintain their original color.

▶ WOOD RAILINGS HAVE A NUMBER of advantages: They are pleasant to grip even in very hot or cold weather, can take on a variety of profiles, are suitable for older homes, and can offer historic styling. Here the same rail is used in the second-floor pocket deck as on the long deck, bringing visual harmony to the two parts of the house.

Defining Railings

THE TERM "RAILING" is used interchangeably, but depending on where the railing falls, it is either a guardrail or a handrail. Building codes make this distinction clear in the regulations that apply to each. Check your local building code for specific requirements.

Guardrails surround a raised deck and are commonly 36 in. above the deck floor. **Handrails** follow alongside a stairway, with their height measured vertically from the nosing (the outer edge of the step's overhang) so that it falls within a range prescribed by building codes, generally about 32 in. to 36 in. Handrails must have a graspable profile to grip while climbing the stair, whereas guardrails need not be designed for gripping.

The area between the railings and deck or stairway is the **balustrade** and may be composed of closely spaced horizontal or vertical members, or it can be built as a low, solid wall, sometimes termed a **knee wall**. Knee walls must include scuppers—gaps for the water to drain out.

The spacing of the individual balusters must be close enough to prevent a 4-in.-diameter or larger ball from passing through. The gap between the balustrade and the steps cannot be larger than a 6-in.-diameter ball.

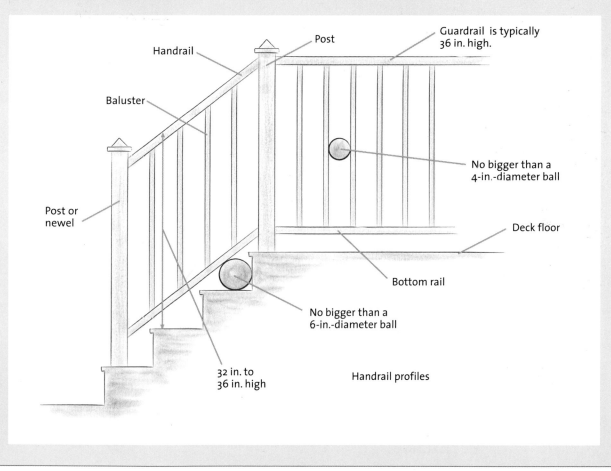

Handrail

Post

Guardrail is typically 36 in. high.

Baluster

No bigger than a 4-in.-diameter ball

Post or newel

Deck floor

Bottom rail

No bigger than a 6-in.-diameter ball

32 in. to 36 in. high

Handrail profiles

▶ SHAPED LIKE THE BATTLEMENTS of a castle, this deck features solidly shingled corners interspersed with a wood railing. The corners anchor the railing system visually as well as structurally, making it especially sturdy, which is critical for second-level decks.

▶ NATURAL WOOD RAILINGS would look too heavy and create too much contrast with this white-washed home, so they've been painted. Cedar or pressure-treated lumber is typically used for painted railings, and maintenance is key; you don't want water to stand on painted wood, so slant the top rail a little (as was done here) if it is made of a single plank, or shape the top of the rail to shed water.

Wood Balustrade Designs

THERE IS AN UNLIMITED VARIETY of designs for wood balustrades, which can add distinctive style to any deck. As long as the spacing between the balusters meets building code requirements, the pieces can be placed vertically, horizontally, or on the diagonal. Balustrades can be made of individual 1½-in. by 1½-in. balusters set in a row or be arranged with more ornate turned balusters or boards cut with a decorative profile. Balustrades are constructed in sections between upright posts that secure the balustrade to the deck framing. These look best and are sturdier when there is no more than 8 ft. of balustrade between posts.

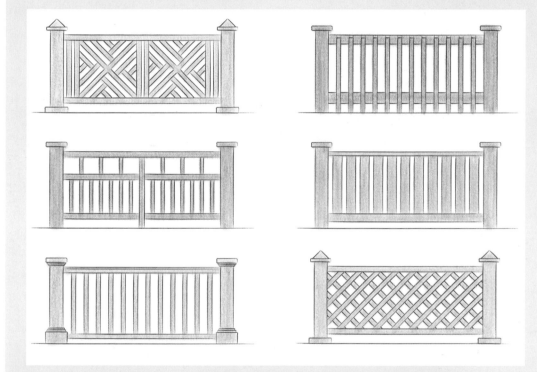

◀THE ALTERNATING RHYTHM to this railing must be planned in advance so that the design fits into the length of the railing; an abrupt ending in the middle of one of the H-shaped panels would look like a mistake. This holds true for any deck that has a row of individual panels.

▶CURVED TOP AND BOTTOM RAILINGS formed of short sections of wood plank follow the gentle curve of this second-story deck that extends this home's footprint toward the water. Tying the ends in to the posts holding up the roof makes the railing more secure.

▼DESIGNED BY A CARPENTER for his own home, this railing frame is made of clear cedar and the spindles are ¹⁄₂-in. black pipe held in place with wooden dowels. With few exposed fasteners, there are fewer places for staining and rotting.

◀EQUALLY SPACED POSTS and balustrade panels with a medallion of sorts add a little spice to this railing pattern. The white rail contrasts with the vivid blues and greens of the natural surroundings and the pink and purple palette of the plants.

◄GOING BEYOND STRICT geometric shapes, this raised deck undulates above a supporting stone wall, forming pockets to stand within and view the terrain below. The sinuous railing echoes the deck's curve but is given further architectural interest through the profile of the balusters, which undulate vertically.

BALUSTERS

Taking a cue from more decorative porch railings, the individual balusters that make up a deck's balustrade need not be just simple 2x2s.

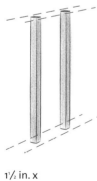

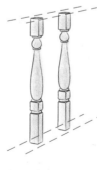

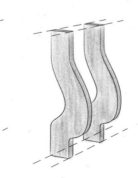

1½ in. x
1½ in. square

Turned

Set flat with
decorative
cutouts

Cut with a curvy
profile from
2x6 boards

▶USING A SOLID WALL AS RAILING makes a deck feel like part of the house—more like a porch without a roof. This railing is faced with the same clapboard and white trim as the house.

▼THIS HARMONIOUSLY DESIGNED deck features a solid railing made of the same shingled siding as that on the house, and the tapered columns are consistent with the prominent roof angles as well as the slanted cuts at the sides of the scuppers.

▲ A SHINGLED KNEE WALL forms the low, curved railing on this lofty deck built at treetop level. An enclosed balustrade offers more security for high-up decks like this and also serves as a windbreak.

◄ GLASS RAILING SYSTEMS are great for providing an unimpeded view and in this case, a wind-screen, but they are pricey and need to be kept clean. This type of railing style is really more of a non-style and can complement any house.

▶ A TRANSPARENT BALUSTRADE is created by aircraft cable stretched horizontally between steel uprights, with a wooden top rail on this raised deck. These cables are readily available at specialty hardware and stair and railing fabricators. The metal posts extend below the deck at the edge and are lag-bolted into the rim joist for stability and secure attachment.

ALTERNATIVES TO WOOD RAILINGS

There are many alternatives to wood railings, notably balustrades made up of pipe railing, wrought iron, aircraft cable, wire mesh, or glass or acrylic panels.

Painted steel or copper tubing

Galvanized steel cable

Painted steel mesh

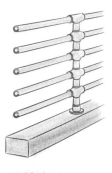

Acrylic or glass panels

Welded steel tubing

▲ THE USE OF UNUSUAL MATERIALS—like wire mesh in a wooden frame—and unexpected elements, such as the white columns, add visual interest to this deck. The rail is notched around the column for stability.

◄ NAUTICAL IN FEEL, this pipe railing is well suited to its shoreline locale. Pipe railing has several advantages: It's fairly inexpensive to build, can be fabricated off-site and assembled on-site, can be painted any color, and weathers well.

▲ THERE IS CRISP ARCHITECTURAL GEOMETRY at work in this contemporary railing composed of tightly spaced horizontal steel cables. The solid-wood posts are interspersed at regular intervals by thinner metal uprights, and a floorboard at each wood post running perpendicular to the rest of the decking marks the same intervals in the deck. Little details like this make a thoughtful difference in the design.

STAIRS

◄ BRIDGING TWO REGIONS of the house, this utilitarian stairway makes a straight run from a deck to a graveled patio with open risers, which are advantageous because water, leaves, and other debris can't accumulate.

► THESE CASCADING STAIRS are used to architecturally link three levels of the house, and are wide and shallow enough to linger on comfortably, creating additional subspaces and seating where guests can congregate during large parties.

Comfortable Stairs

THE BUILDING CODES governing stairs at decks are the same as for interior stairs. For utilitarian stairs descending a full story from the deck to the ground, basic dimensions of tread and riser can follow the range of maximums and minimums required by the code. But for stairs that are designed to be integrated into level changes of multiple decks, or for those that are to be more decorative or prominent, the relationship between tread and riser is more comfortable when it is not so steep. Deeper treads and shallower risers gently encourage a slower step or might offer a place to pause on a landing. For an outdoor stair, a comfortable relationship of tread to riser is a 6-in. to 7-in. riser height with a 10-in. to 12-in. tread depth. As a major traffic pathway, stairs need to be at least 3 ft. wide, but it's even better if they're 5 ft. or wider, allowing two to walk together.

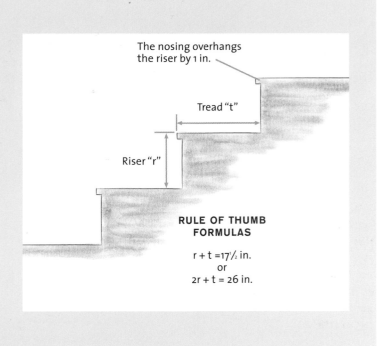

The nosing overhangs the riser by 1 in.

Tread "t"

Riser "r"

RULE OF THUMB FORMULAS

$r + t = 17\frac{1}{2}$ in.
or
$2r + t = 26$ in.

◀ WITH ONLY THREE SHALLOW risers needed to get from the deck to the lawn, no surrounding guardrail is necessary, which means the panoramic view can be enjoyed in all its glory without interruptions.

▲ TAKING A 90-DEGREE TURN at a landing inserts a pause in ascending or descending a longer flight of stairs, and in a small area makes it easier to negotiate the change in elevation. This maze of a deck incorporates several landings—some that serve as decks themselves and others that change the direction of the stair.

▶ IN KEEPING WITH the surrounding landscapte, these rustic stairs built of peeled and split logs make a perfect transition from deck to landscape.

◄ THINK OF A RAMP as an "architectural hill" rather than as a blot on the landscape, and this one blends in naturally while making it a breeze to access the deck in a wheelchair or to push a grill or stroller onto it.

Ramps

THE AMERICANS with Disabilities Act (ADA) has made it a requirement to design new stores, apartment houses, and offices in a manner that ensures they're accessible to individuals with mobility and sensory difficulties. Although no such requirement exists for private residences, incorporating a ramp into deck design can be useful, not only for family members or guests in wheelchairs but also for wheeling grills, strollers, and other items up to a deck. Ramps are defined by their slope, a ratio between the number of inches in vertical rise per number of inches in horizontal run. The ADA requires a 1:12 slope, but for a private home, a steeper ramp (up to 1:8) also is acceptable.

◄ THE 45-DEGREE ANGLES OF THIS HOUSE are reflected in the turn of the deck's stair as it rounds the corner of the house. Changing the direction of the planking is a good idea to subtly signal a change in elevation to someone walking along.

Screens and Skirting

Trimming the deck with a skirtboard and/or a lattice screening finishes it to the same degree as the house by concealing the less elegant framing and the shadowy space beneath a raised deck.

The skirtboard runs horizontally beneath the overhanging deck boards. This can be painted to match the trim of the house's corner boards or other trim pieces, or it can match the species of the deck floor and balustrade. Either way, it should be wide enough to hide the rough framing of the deck's undercarriage.

Screening the space under the deck is generally done with closely spaced boards or a lattice, hung either diagonally or at right angles to the skirt. Covering the void helps to keep animals and debris out from under the deck. Lattice is generally bought in sections at lumberyards or home centers and can be painted or left natural. Do not let the bottom edge of the lattice touch the ground or it will get wet and begin to rot. Bordering the bottom edge of the screening with another horizontal board presents a more finished look.

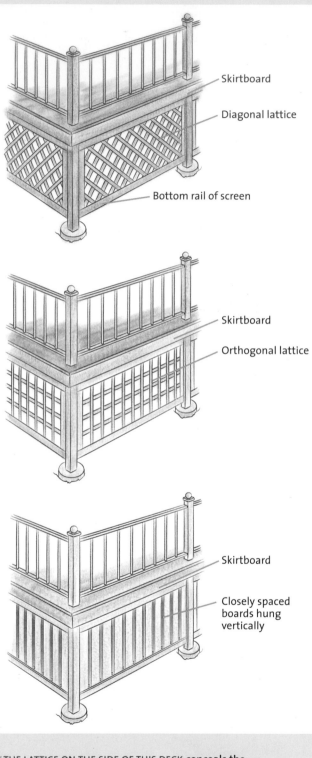

Skirtboard

Diagonal lattice

Bottom rail of screen

Skirtboard

Orthogonal lattice

Skirtboard

Closely spaced boards hung vertically

◄ THE LATTICE ON THE SIDE OF THIS DECK conceals the framing and helps keep varmints from taking up residence underneath. The same lattice is echoed in the balcony railing above.

▲ PLANTERS FORM THE GUARDRAIL on this expansive deck, which uses white lattice as screening and as a backdrop to highlight the unique twin stairs. Situating the stairs at an unusual angle to each other creates a sense of drama and sophistication that a straight stair would not.

◀ SOMETIMES MOTHER NATURE DICTATES the placement of our man-made embellishments—here the position of a beautiful, ivy-covered tree determined the location of these stairs, which were forced to jog over from the edge of the top deck. The stairs have solid risers (the vertical portion between each tread), which hide the view of the space under the upper deck and give the stair a more substantial feel.

▶ BRINGING THE CONVERSATION pit from the living room to the deck is a great idea for an outdoor room. This brick fire pit was built into a sunken deck enclosure. The semicircular built-in bench is made up of short, straight planks cut to form the curve.

◀ A COMBINATION OF BUILT-IN and freestanding furniture fills out this shady corner, giving it a real sense of enclosure, like an open-air living room. Cushions can be covered with water-repellent fabric but still shouldn't be left outside or they'll become sodden and rot. If cushions will be out all the time, they should be made of special fabrics specifically designed for outdoor use.

Built-In Benches

A BUILT-IN BENCH is a welcome amenity to any deck. Consider the views and the function of any built-in furniture as you determine where to place a bench and whether it should have a back or be backless. A bench placed by the door might be a convenient spot to remove muddy shoes or put down the groceries while fumbling for the keys. Built-in benches surrounding a picnic table create a permanent corner for designated dining. And long, backless benches that wrap the perimeter of a low deck are great for large gatherings, allowing guests to face the house or the view beyond.

To ensure comfortable seating, pay careful attention to the distance from the seat edge to the deck floor and from seat edge to seat back. The seat should be 15 in. to 16 in. off the floor, and the seat depth should be no less than 16 in. but no deeper than 24 in. if the bench has a back.

▲ THESE BACKLESS BUILT-IN BENCHES are designed to multitask: They define the perimeter of the low deck; they're wide enough for a sunbather to stretch out on; and they allow seating in either direction depending on the activity—taking in the view or socializing on the deck.

◄ IN THIS UNDERSTATED BUILT-IN eating area, the inset of the deck within the roof overhang makes a protected spot just outside the door. Built-in benches need to be sanded smooth periodically to avoid splinters. Note the electrical outlet—it's a waterproof type made specifically for exterior use.

◄A CONTINUOUS BENCH ZIGZAGS around the perimeter of this angular deck. The bench is made up of the same planks as the deck floor, only turned on their sides. Slightly pitching the top surface of the guardrail helps it to shed water. The railing also conceals tiny light fixtures.

▼ALTHOUGH THESE BENCHES ARE NOT ATTACHED to the decking, they are heavy enough to withstand high wind on this rooftop deck and are designed to fit in front of the intervals of lattice. The cushions are used seasonally and are inexpensive.

◀ THIS CIRCULAR, BUILT-IN BENCH makes a convivial and intimate spot around the fire pit at cook-out time. The colorful cushions are neatly attached with tabs so they won't shift or blow away.

Outdoor Storage

GRILL ACCESSORIES, citronella candles, and bench cushions are most useful when kept close at hand, so it's worth designating storage for them on the deck.

Outdoor storage needs to be easily accessible and attractive, but primarily it needs to be waterproof. A box tucked into the side of a stair landing or inside a bench is less conspicuous than a freestanding shed on a deck, but make sure the unit has a solid top to shed water and a perforated bottom to drain any water that seeps in. If you're building a new deck, storage can be incorporated into the design in the form of a built-in chest or of subdeck compartments as shown here. Consider a lockable unit for expensive accessories, hazardous items, or long-term storage.

▲ A WIRE BASKET UNDER A LID that's part of the decking is well ventilated—a clever and handy solution to storage for hoses and other outdoor tools.

◀INSTEAD OF A LAWN, dense plantings ring this deck, making it feel like a clearing in the forest. The low wooden walls do double duty as both railings and seating areas. The wide steps offer additional places to perch.

Integrating Plants

BRIGHT AND SUNNY DECKS are ideal spots for plants and flowers to flourish. Integrating plants with your deck furnishings will increase the sense of connection with nature, add color and scent, and even provide fresh herbs and produce.

While freestanding pots offer mobility, built-in planters can be integrated into a deck's railings or benches, providing creative design opportunities and an alternative to guardrails.

Regardless of the type of planters, care must be taken with species selection and adequate watering because the ambient temperature on an unshaded deck is much hotter than on a lawn.

▶THIS LARGE DECK is divided into two distinct sections by a long built-in that marks the level change—there's a bench on one side and a planter on the other that takes the place of a deck rail. Potted plants also have been set at intervals along the bench, implying different seating areas.

▲THE BENCHES SURROUNDING the room-size portion of this deck are just the right height for perching or putting up one's feet, and planters at the edges add a touch of color to the weathered decking. Generously sized and oriented toward the view, this part of the deck is the main area for congregating.

◀YOU MIGHT NOT NEED A guardrail if a substantial planter can define the edge of the deck. Here three rows of planter boxes ensure a riot of seasonal color. Air and water circulation are important factors in planter design, so they should be built from naturally rot-resistant or pressure-treated woods.

Shade and Shelter

DECKS SHOULD BE ORIENTED TO GATHER AS MUCH SUN as possible, but they are most enjoyable if they provide the option of shade. Arbors, trellises, and pergolas do this while increasing the sense of shelter and security on a deck. Overhead structures also add a vertical dimension to an otherwise horizontal deck and help create a sequence of spatial experiences in our outdoor rooms, dividing and defining different areas.

Of course, positioning your deck to take advantage of natural shade can be the simplest approach, and there are other shady devices such as awnings and umbrellas that provide a less permanent solution.

▲ THE LYRICAL, ARCHED BEAMS of this picturesque arbor tie in thematically with the circles in the latticework, as well as to the arched doorway leading into the house (at right). For a little aromatherapy on the deck, choose a fragrant plant or vine, such as the wisteria used here.

▲SURROUNDED BY WOODS, this deck on the east side of the house has great natural shade; there's partial shade by lunchtime and full shade by dinner. In the winter, there's plenty of natural light because the surrounding trees lose their leaves, warming the deck and the house naturally.

◄THIS DECK IS ONE STEP FROM BECOMING A PORCH— you'd just have to sheath the rafters of the pergola and voila! When the overhead members of a pergola slope, they are called rafters rather than joists, as they mimic the skeletal form of a virtual roof rather than a flat ceiling. The deck edge zigzags, making each corner of it unique and offering many zones to furnish and use.

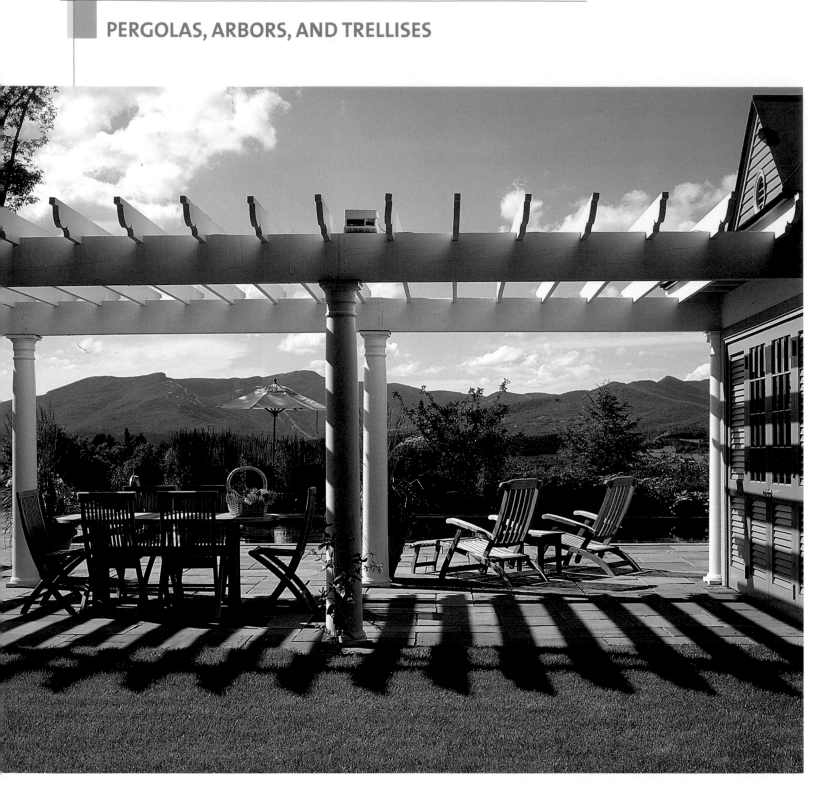

▲ THE CONNECTION BETWEEN HOUSE AND GARDEN is framed by a formal overhead pergola at this shady poolside spot. The play of light and shadow creates a ribbon of virtual texture on the ground, adding another pattern to the landscaping and one that changes during the course of the day.

THIS DECK ENTRANCE topped by a pergola was designed in concert with the architecture of the house and is an artful example of how a series of small spaces can be thoughtfully connected to provide an evocative transition as you move from one space to the next.

▼ HAVING DISTINCT ZONES within a commodious deck reduces the scale so it doesn't give the impression of one large platform but rather a series of areas for different uses—such as grilling, sitting, napping, or eating. A portion of this deck juts out like a stage onto the lawn, and the simple pergola acts as the proscenium defining this particular portion of the deck.

◀ A CANOPY EFFECT is created by the overhead arbor that shades this seat. Arched beams support a parade of purlins, and the entire structure is freestanding and can be moved to another spot periodically for a change in view. The teak bench structure weathers to a lovely silver gray.

▲ A PERGOLA OFFERS A SENSE of shelter but is open to the sun and stars. Here six unadorned posts support three beams that span the width of this simple structure, providing shade, intimacy, and a sense of verticality to this platform deck. The pergola also plays host to a hammock and hanging plants.

► THIS UNIQUE OVERHEAD structure is composed of beams reaching out from the house, with a canopy of green from the trees creating a light-filtering infill between. Clad in the same clapboard siding, the beams cleverly incorporate light fixtures for nighttime use.

Trellis, Arbor, or Pergola?

TRELLIS DESCRIBES the armature constructed from slender wooden members that are designed for plants to grow against or over. A trellis can be mounted vertically against a wall or freestanding, or can be used horizontally as the ceiling plane of an arbor.

An arbor is an outdoor room created by a freestanding three-dimensional structure made of posts and overhead joists (when they are horizontal) or rafters (when they slope). An arbor is meant to inhabit for the enjoyment of a shady spot.

A Pergola is an arbor that is attached to the house, like an open-air arcade. It provides shade on a walkway as well as shades the house's windows and glass doors from the sun's hot glare in the summer, while permitting the lower winter sun to reach the interior.

TRELLIS
In the form of a vertical lattice.

BRISE-SOLEIL
A type of trellis that shades a window with slender fins.

Interlocking joists with decorative tails

Arched lattice panel

Post

Lattice

ARBOR
An arched beam supports an overhead trellis.

PERGOLA
Interlocking joists with decorative tails

▶ THIS SUMMERY ENCLOSURE is a simple open-air booth with lattice panels at the sides. Cut with a decorative shape at the ends, the joists are topped at right angles by purlins, the smaller square pieces of wood that add another layer of shading and texture to this enclosure.

◀ THE BOARDWALK-LIKE SECTION of this deck is mirrored above by a pergola extending from the roof of the house. Beyond, the pergola widens just as the deck below it does. The L of the deck surrounds a water garden that reflects light back up into the glass walls of the house. Without the pergola, there would be too much glare to enjoy the approach to this house.

▲ A ROOFTOP DECK like this is prime real estate in a city, especially during the summer. The roll-down shades over the latticework render complete privacy from the adjacent building, and the latticed arbor provides shade and a haven for plants and residents alike. Sleepers (wood planks laid horizontally at wide intervals) under a deck floor will raise the deck above a hot, asphalt roof without penetrating the waterproof membrane.

Privacy Screens

WHEN NEIGHBORS ARE TOO CLOSE for comfort, or if there's a less than lovely view, consider using a privacy screen. Privacy screening is not quite a fence, but rather a semitransparent wall that allows breezes in, while filtering the view. Lattice set between posts is the simplest screening, but more elaborate configurations can be made incorporating benches and overhead trellises.

OTHER SHADY DEVICES

▲ THIS EXPANSIVE DECK MAKES WAY for nature by accommodating three large trees. The holes in the deck are large enough to allow movement, growth, and water absorption. The trees provide natural shade in the summer, while allowing solar heat to penetrate the house when they lose their leaves in the winter.

◄ WHILE THE PERGOLA ATTACHED to this house adds architectural interest and marks a transitional area between house and deck, the large umbrella provides the shade and visually anchors the deck in the landscape.

A DEEP, OVERHANGING ROOF provides a welcome shadow at the edges of the house, shading the deck and the adjacent window. In the winter, when the sun angles are lower, sunlight will penetrate the house through the windows, providing natural heat.

Fabric Awnings

IN ADDITION TO PROVIDING uninterrupted shade, awnings can also direct rain off a deck, making them a useful alternative to open-air arbors or pergolas. Removable or retractable awnings are a good option in colder climates because they allow the sun to reach any windows off the deck in cooler months, thus maximizing heat and sunlight. There are coated fabrics made specifically for awnings, similar to those used for sunshade umbrellas; they are ideal for outdoor use but are heavy and should be fabricated by a specialist. Alternatively, thin nylon and other synthetic materials, while not as durable, can be easily sewn and attached with grommets to the substructure of a wood or metal frame.

THIS DECK EMPLOYS A FABRIC AWNING that filters light and moves with the breeze, creating a fluid roof. This can be taken down after the summer and repaired and replaced easily.

Maximizing the View

P ART OF THE ALLURE OF SITTING OUTSIDE is taking in the views provided by the natural surroundings. Whether your house has an open view to the water, a serene mountain vista, or simply looks into a yard or garden, a deck should be oriented to optimize views of the landscape.

In addition to proper orientation, you should consider architectural details that can further maximize the view. Sometimes this means ensuring that nothing will obstruct a grand panoramic view; however, many views are best enjoyed when they are directed and framed by something in the foreground or middle ground. Regardless of what your landscape has to offer, careful planning can make the most of it, providing your deck with pleasing views that enhance the outdoor experience.

◄ THE VIEW FROM A DECK isn't always a spectacular vista; a more restrained foreground view of a garden or woodland is much more typical of a suburban deck and can be just as inspiring. Limiting railings as much as permitted will put the viewer into the landscape instead of being just a passive observer.

◀THE VIEW HERE is so captivating that two parts of the deck are designed to take in its splendor; a dock runs from the main deck to another section of raftlike decking in the water. The raft adds a foreground layer to the scene, keeping the view beyond in relative proportion and lending perspective to the sweeping panorama.

▼ORIENTED TO THE WEST, this deck is perched on the side of a bluff, creating the sense that it's reaching right into the landscape and its stunning views. While a western orientation offers breathtaking sunsets, it can also mean a lot of glare when the sun is at its brightest, so for maximum comfort and utility, some type of shading device should be included.

► IF SITE AND BUDGET ALLOW, having decks on more than one side of the house truly maximizes the available views while offering a choice of sun and shade throughout the day. This tall house in the mountains has decks shooting out from all sides, granting views in multiple directions from four different levels.

◄ A DECK WITH A WATER VIEW is subject to the prevailing winds, and this one is sheltered by the Ls of the house. The edge of the deck mirrors the horizon line of the water, and the unobstructed view makes for good bird and boat watching.

◄ THIS LONG DECK runs along the length of the house, offering an extensive overview of the woods and water below, while also creating specific zones, like the seating area, where a specific part of the view can be focused on and enjoyed in detail.

The Cone of Vision

WE CAN ALL ADMIRE A PANORAMIC VIEW, **especially when sitting on a deck overlooking the mountains or the ocean. But our viewpoint is defined by our "cone of vision," the measurable amount of view that we can take in without moving our heads. An imaginary cone with a 60-degree angle defines this view, which is what we can see clearly without relying on our peripheral vision. So, when planning scenic overlooks from a deck, be aware that you can frame smaller snapshot views bordered by trees or other obstructions.**

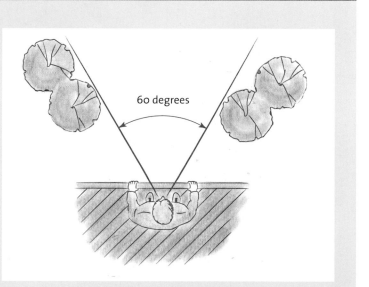

60 degrees

▲THIS FRONT-ROW SEAT TO THE BEST VIEW in the house is architecturally highlighted by the step down from the main deck. The cut ends of the decking at the step are capped by a perpendicular board that protects the ends and makes a neat edge that signals the step. The sheer railing allows for relatively unobstructed enjoyment of the water and horizon.

◄THE SHORELINE VIEW IS FRAMED by this large arch on a second-level deck, where the crisscrossing rafters of the overhead structure create a virtual roof that adds a sense of privacy to this aerie.

◄THIS DECK TAKES ADVANTAGE of the stunning view from many different angles; the expansive pool-side deck has a panoramic view out to the bay and islands, and from the shady cool of a covered porch, another view is framed through the posts that extend along the railing.

Deck and Patio Combinations

COMBINATION DECK/PATIO extends the outdoor living space just as an individual deck or patio would, but it can be more interesting than a single large area of either. Because a deck leads to the landscape and a patio actually sits within it, combining these elements allows you to make the transition from indoors to outdoors on multiple, fluid levels.

This combination approach can be appropriate in any number of situations, such as when the ground slopes dramatically up or down from the house, or when the house has exits at different levels, each leading to an outdoor space. Or you may simply want some variety to accommodate different activity zones. Whether your property is large enough to incorporate several expansive outdoor rooms or is more modest, deck and patio combinations can offer distinct spaces and options.

▼ THIS APPEALING TERRACE is tucked in between the house and the hill rising up behind the overlooking deck. The vertical planes of the stone retaining wall and the curved deck railing above it provide the main texture of this design, responding to and reflecting the steep site.

A SPIRAL STAIRCASE is a good design solution when there's no room for a large staircase, and this one provides visual interest while acting as a sinuous connection between the second-story deck and the small dining patio below.

Spiral Stair

ECAUSE THE TREADS OF A SPIRAL STAIR are cantilevered out from a center post, these corkscrew stairs are very handy when a conventional stair won't fit or when you want the landings at the top and bottom of the flight of stairs to be aligned. For exterior use at a two-tiered deck or rooftop terrace, a manufactured spiral stair is easy to install—a small concrete foundation and a secure attachment at the top landing are all you need to secure the stairway. The smallest-diameter spiral stair that is comfortable to ascend or descend is 48 in.

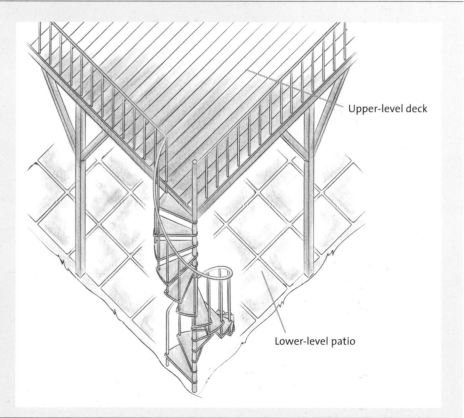

Upper-level deck

Lower-level patio

▲THIS INSPIRED DECK AND PATIO combination is a study in transitions and contrasts. A few pavers in the middle of the patio were removed to make a planting bed, an unexpected surprise in the middle of this grassy lawn. Grass radiates cooler air while heat radiates off the stone portion to create microclimates within the larger space.

▲THE ARCH FRAMES THE VIEW distinctively from both sides—from within the arch there's a long view of the shallow deck and steps, the patio and yard, and the woods out back; from the yard the view through the arch is to a stone wall and wooded area beyond.

▶FROM THE FRONT OF THE HOUSE, shallow wooden steps traverse the landscape down to a small patio. The bottom two treads are more eccentric in shape, subtly turning the path of the stair in a winding fashion toward the monumental arch.

▲ AT BEACHFRONT HOUSES LIKE THIS, a stone patio often buffers the approaching high tides, while the wooden decks are a continuation of the interior family rooms. Mixing different shades of the same color of stone, in this case, gray, makes for an appealing patio design.

◄ THE ROUND BRICK PATIO (right) matches the material of the house, but if it were used as the only paving material, this backyard would feel like an urban court-yard. Instead, the owners opted to use the patio for a specific focal point, with a round wooden bench at the edge.

Patios

Like a deck, a patio allows us to take advantage of all that the great outdoors has to offer, while expanding the useful space of our abodes. Patios have evolved from mere concrete slabs into sophisticated outdoor rooms, ranging from brick courtyards to urban rooftop respites to luxurious poolside havens.

A patio can be attached to the house or placed at a distance, and can accommodate a range of activities, including dining, recreation, and quiet relaxation. Budget, lifestyle, and property dictate what type of patio will be most feasible and useful; energetic hosts might choose a large, multifaceted patio with a range of dining and seating areas, while for others, a small flagstone patch nestled in a garden would provide the perfect spot for quiet reading or reflection.

Regardless of the type of patio you choose to build, there are many architectural considerations; site, style, and materials are key. Once the basics have been decided, there are many other practical and aesthetic features to deliberate: Will steps, walls, or fences be part of the plan? Do you want any overhead structures for shade? Should there be added elements and focal points, such as fireplaces, outdoor kitchens, or water features?

◄ DYNAMIC SWIRLING PATTERNS and undulating motion are the hallmarks of this exotic courtyard patio. Paved in slate and ochre stone, it also features a blue glass mosaic that lends drama and a personalized flair to the design. The chairs and decorative railings above continue the wavy theme.

Patio Types

With the array of paving materials available, patio design can be as traditional or imaginative as you desire. But regardless of style, the majority of patios fall into one of the following categories.

An attached patio extends a house into the landscape and can be furnished like a room. A freestanding patio is generally sited to capitalize on a particular aspect of the landscape, such as a garden or a captivating view. A rooftop or balcony patio, most frequently found in urban landscapes, creates outdoor space when there's none to be had at ground level. A courtyard patio unites the wings of the house and is often designed as part of the main living space. And finally, a poolside patio focuses on recreation and entertainment. The type of patio you build should work in conjunction with your house, landscape, and lifestyle to ensure the most useful and pleasing outdoor space.

▼THIS ATTACHED STONE PATIO is positioned to soak up the sun's radiant heat, and while the surface can be hot in the summer, it's comfortably warm in the autumn and spring, maximizing its seasonal use. Although small, the patio provides plenty of room for outdoor lounging and a pleasing transition between house and lawn.

▲ BECAUSE BALCONY AND ROOFTOP PATIOS are set well above ground level, they have some special requirements. This Spanish-style balcony patio rests atop a rounded room, so waterproofing the surface under the paving is essential. Also, the entire patio needs to slope at least ¼ in. per foot to allow water drainage.

◄ FREESTANDING PATIOS ARE A GOOD OPTION when the surrounding ground is soft or sandy, and this patio makes the most of a seaside spot, providing a seating area in the garden. Composed of gravel, which can be easily replenished as needed, the patio is lined with Belgian block edging that helps contain the gravel while adding visual interest.

▶ SURROUNDED BY A VARIETY of lush plantings, this freestanding brick patio acts as a focal point in the garden. The sundial is a traditional garden accent, but it's important to keep in mind that any accessory exposed to the elements will deteriorate quickly if it's not of good quality and designed for outdoor use.

PATIO TYPES

PATIO ON GRADE
Laid directly onto the level of the ground with no intervening steps from grass to patio. A fairly level site is required.

RAISED PATIO
Sits a few steps up from the surrounding yard and built so that one can go directly from the house onto the patio without any stairs. Also used with a sloping yard where the first floor of the house is high above the surrounding grade.

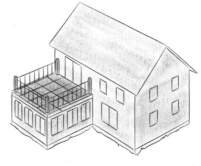

ROOFTOP PATIO
Set on top of the flat-roofed portion of a house. The roof framing of this patio must be designed to support heavy patio materials, such as concrete and stone.

POOLSIDE PATIO
The paved area immediately around a pool. Designed to withstand chlorinated water.

◄ STURDY, SQUARED-OFF COLUMNS anchor this hybrid patio and porch and support a unique overhead roof structure. Farther down the hill a freestanding patio of the same stone material is built out to face the mountains.

▼ NATURAL STONES HAVE MORE TEXTURE than cut or polished stone pavers, so wet feet won't slip as easily, making them ideal for pool patios. The large, irregular stones surrounding this poolside patio have wide spaces between them that let the grass grow through, creating a natural look that blends nicely into this rustic landscape.

◄ A COLORFUL ROOFTOP PATIO transforms what could have been a strictly utilitarian space (the stairs lead to a water tank) into an outdoor room with a view. The wider the mortar joints, the less precise you need to be about fitting irregular stones, making this type of patio a good project for do-it-yourselfers.

◄ THIS HOUSE FEATURES TWO PATIOS with very different functions; although spatially disjointed, they're visually connected by corresponding style and materials. The courtyard patio separates the garage from the house while providing a turnaround for cars, and the freestanding patio, which is cleverly sunk into an existing slope, provides a pleasant dining spot.

◄ THE NATURAL STONE FOUNDATION WALL of the house is reflected in the more refined stone that's used in the attached patio, creating a natural flow between the two. The patio further complements the house by following its contour; this design also maximizes the panoramic view.

▼ THIS STRIKING DESIGN EMPLOYS a combination of angular symmetry and contrasting curves to produce a dramatic poolside patio. The interesting color variation in the pavers prevents the layout from looking too artificial. Rougher-textured stones are used at the lip of the pool and spa for both traction and a decorative border.

Patio Materials

MATERIAL SELECTION HAS A BIG IMPACT on a patio's style. The most common patio materials are brick, stone, rock or gravel, concrete, and tile. Each has unique qualities that lend themselves to different types of designs, and they can be used in combination for added depth and texture. Brick, for instance, has an air of tradition, but it can be used in both very formal and very rustic designs. The natural beauty of stone promotes the use of regional materials to complement the local architecture. Rocks and gravel can be used loose for an informal feel, and some types can be set in mortar to create intricate mosaic patterns. Versatile, inexpensive concrete can either be poured in place or cast into varied-shape pavers that mimic other materials. Tile is particularly alluring, and although it has a rustic feel, it works well in either formal or casual settings.

In addition to pure aesthetics, when designing a patio that works for you, you'll also need to consider price, availability, and which materials can be integrated harmoniously with your house and property.

▼ MULTICOLORED CONCRETE PAVERS laid in varying patterns add dimension and flair to this refined patio. Edging the patio with multiple layers—plantings, stone wall, and wooden baluster—creates much more visual interest than a single material would.

▲ IN A DELIBERATE ATTEMPT to create an indistinct shape for this patio, slabs of limestone and strips of sod do a positive/negative dance as they weave at the margins of this deck. Limestone makes a good patio material, with edges that soften over time, creating a natural feel.

◄ THE GRAVEL "RAFT" afloat in a pond of pebbles creates a focal point in this alluring patio area. The raised platform defines a seating area within the larger space of patio and landscape. Gravel is a permeable material that allows water to soak into the earth, making it a good material in garden settings or in areas with trees nearby.

BRICK

▲ A PORCH OR DECK IS an extension of a house, but a patio is more an extension of the yard. When space permits, it's possible to create more than one patio area, as seen at this home, which has a pair of brick outdoor zones. One was placed in a sunny spot just steps down from the porch, the other in a shadier garden area at the edge of the woods.

▲ LINING THE EDGES OF PATIO STEPS accentuates them and calls attention to the change in level—an important safety feature. Here, an expansive patio is edged in railroad ties to visually break up what could otherwise be an overwhelming sea of brick. The planting bed situated between two sets of steps creates a colorful focal point.

Brick Paving

BRICK IS A COMMON MATERIAL **for paving patios and walk-ways and comes in a huge range of colors, textures, and shapes that can be used in an infinite number of patterns. There are several kinds of brick that can be used on patios. Paving bricks are fired at very high temperatures and last longer than common brick, which is usually used for walls, though it can be used for paving in mild climates. Vintage or used brick looks nicely weathered from the beginning and blends well with plant materials. It can be mixed with granite edging or other stone pavers, as well as wood timbers.**

Brick is laid either on a tamped sand base or set onto a concrete slab and mortared in place. In most paving patterns, bricks are put down with the widest face showing; the narrower sides and edges are used for borders and for special design applications. Bricks can be laid tightly together or with space between, showing grass, moss, or a wide mortar joint. Regardless, the surface can become moldy and thus slippery if it's in a damp, shady area and will have to be cleaned regularly.

▲IN THIS COOL, SHADY SPOT topped by a rustic arbor, the brick patio is laid in a running bond pattern; the spacious fit of the bricks is forgiving when the ground heaves in colder months.

◀THE LIVELY, HERRINGBONE pattern seen here is easy to lay once it's established at one edge or starting point. It's complemented by the more basic running bond pattern in the wall, which was kept low so as not to obstruct the view. Note the clever solution for dealing with runoff water—the downspout has an extender that removes it below the elevation of the patio.

▶ SETTING THIS BASKETWEAVE PATTERN in sand rather than mortar creates a more informal look. The bricks don't need to be dead level when they're set in sand, allowing for more variation in the natural topography of a site.

▼ BRICK CAN BE AN ALTERNATIVE to the ubiquitous bluestone pool patio. Bricks are visually appealing against the green grass and blue water, and they blend well with the landscaping. Chlorine stains anything, so keep that in mind when choosing materials.

BRICK PAVING PATTERNS

Running bond

Parquet or basketweave

Herringbone

Stack bond

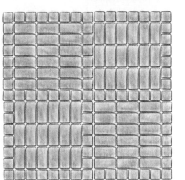

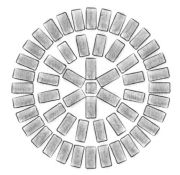

Sectional (like a big checkerboard)

Concentric

▲ PERFECTLY SITUATED to catch the morning sun, this brick courtyard is sandwiched between the garage and the bedroom and just steps off the kitchen, making it a good place to relax with coffee and the morning paper. Like all masonry, brick retains heat, so it will warm up quickly on a chilly morning.

STONE

▲▲ A RADIATING STONE PATTERN punctuated by a circular planting bed with a sundial evokes a meditative path that contrasts nicely with the social seating area it connects to. The clean lines of this pattern require precise craftsmanship and a more liberal budget, but the unique result is a landscaping gem.

▲ THE NATURAL, UNCUT EDGES of these phyllite pavers (in the slate and schist family) quarried by the homeowner give the impression of free-floating islands in a gravelly sea. Casual but dramatic, the patio acts as a focal point in the landscape while still blending well with the rustic surroundings. Since the stones don't have to fit together, this free-form approach allows more leeway in stone selection and assembly.

◄ THIS CASUAL CONFIGURATION of random flagstones makes it easy to install a patio (simply set flat stones into the ground) around existing trees without disturbing their roots. The intermingling of hardscape and landscape generates an organic flow that is complemented by the overhead arbor strewn with vines.

Stone Paving

CUT STONE PAVERS, called flagstones, are large square or rectangular stones, about 2 in. thick, with smooth faces and square edges, although irregular-shaped flagstones are also available. Pavers can be laid in ordered rows or in more random patterns. The types of stone most often used for flagstone are slate, bluestone, and sandstone. Fieldstone and other rough stones look the most natural, but they are uneven in thickness and need to be set carefully to achieve a level patio.

Another type of stone used for paving is stone blocks, or cobbles; these are made of granite and referred to as Belgian block. Because of its uneven surface and expense, Belgian block is most often used in small areas or for edging another material, such as granite, brick, or flagstone.

▲ A SEA OF STONE BLOCKS CAN LOOK MONOLITHIC, but the added pattern of the larger pavers breaks up the expanse on this formal patio. The pathways implied by the block areas lead to a shady place under the arbor.

◀ THE OVERALL DIMENSIONS of this compact patio match the scale and proportions of the adjacent portion of the house, making a cohesive whole of outdoor and indoor spaces. The pavers laid in a neat grid pattern contrast nicely with the more random look of the old stone house.

▲ STONE PAVERS HAVE TO BE MEASURED precisely in an elegant setting like this one, where a clear, curved line is drawn between patio and manicured lawn. On a large patio that is set in mortar, there needs to be a slight slope so that water can run off toward the grass.

▶ USING REGIONAL MATERIALS for paving and planting creates a naturally harmonious effect. Here, large limestone pavers form a patio that meanders through planting beds, and different-height blocks of the same stone add a vertical dimension. Space has been left between the blocks for plants to thrive.

STONE PAVING PATTERNS

Random with cut pavers

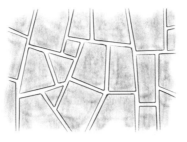
Random with irregular pavers

Regular rows with cut pavers
of equal size

Regular rows with cut pavers
of varying sizes

▼ALTERNATING WIDTHS in the running bond pattern of these bluestone pavers gives a sense of movement to this patio, which winds between the house and shed. Planting beds placed where stone pavers were omitted at the perimeter offers gardeners an accessible bed and brings the plants tableside. When installing your patio, remember to plan for long-term growth in the plantings or use annuals.

Code Considerations

ALTHOUGH PATIOS GENERALLY **aren't covered** by building codes, they may be subject to local zoning codes, which vary by municipality. For instance, towns that limit the total area of developed land surface on a given property may consider the square footage of a patio the same as a building's square footage; others don't count patios at all. In addition, the setback requirements for buildings may also extend to setback requirements for patios, limiting the proximity of your patio to your property line. Knowing what the parameters are for your property before you plan a patio can save you a lot of time, money, and frustration if you end up finding out the hard way.

▲ PATIOS LAID WITH CLOSELY FITTED STONES like this need to be pitched slightly to allow rainwater to run off. The irregularly shaped stones are fitted together in a gentle arc to form a gracious patio that extends along the front of the house. With distinct zones at either end, there's plenty of room for different activities here.

◀ A "BARELY THERE" PATIO like this can evolve and expand over time as you collect rocks from the outer landscape and bring them home. Conforming to the gentle slope of the lawn, this charming patio has the appearance of a naturally occurring rock formation.

ROCK AND GRAVEL

▲ THIS SCULPTURE GARDEN features a stone patio with a seating area abutting a gravel wraparound, which extends the patio area and forms a meditative path. Although the stone patio is permanent, the planter boxes and gravel can be reconfigured or expanded fairly easily if so desired, offering flexibility to this outdoor space.

◀ WHIMSICAL PATIOS WITH DETAILED PATTERNS can be created simply by setting small pebbles in mortar. Here, contrasting colors of the same material show off the craftsman's talent and delicate design sense. While beautiful and unique, pebble mosaics can be labor-intensive and thus expensive; using them solely for accents can cut down on costs.

▲GRAVEL OR PEA STONE PROVIDES a less formal patio, which can be easily expanded at any time with a truckload of additional stones. Although it's difficult to walk barefoot on gravel, it drains well when it rains or snows.

Paving with Rock and Gravel

GRAVEL, FROM WHITE MARBLE CHIPS to ordinary gray pea stones, is a relatively cheap, locally obtainable patio material. Round, tumbled stone gravel is kinder to bare feet than crushed stone, which can have sharp edges. Organic material, such as grass or weeds, should be removed before laying a gravel bed—a depth of 6 in. to 8 in. is ideal. Some type of edging, which can be anything from stone to wood to brick, is needed to contain the bed. Gravel patios are fairly easy to maintain by raking regularly and replenishing annually. They drain well, though they're difficult to shovel in snowy climates.

◀▲ RIVER ROCKS ARE LARGE PEBBLES worn smooth by water over many years, and those used for this mosaic-style patio were locally quarried. The swirling petal patterns created by the colorful rocks set in mortar lend a sense of artistic formality to this sophisticated outdoor room.

▶ THIS STRIKING PATIO features pavers cut on a curve and laced with gravel, which provides far more design flexibility than mortar would. Distinct geometric shapes like this circle demonstrate how a graphic design pattern can be used in paving to direct a gaze, create a focal point, or define a zone in a larger context.

CONCRETE

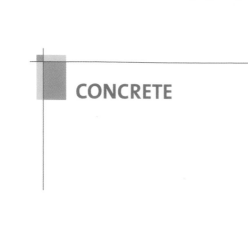

▲ THIS CURVY PATIO EXEMPLIFIES the versatility of concrete. Tinted a warm brown color, the concrete was poured into curved forms and was then stamped with an irregular geometric pattern that mimics stone pavers.

◀ SMALL CONCRETE PAVERS contrast with the broad and tall concrete wall on this patio, while the streaming horizontal vine adds dimension and a dramatic splash of color. Large expanses of concrete may need control joints or expansion joints to direct any cracking as the material shrinks and expands; this holds true for both horizontal slabs and vertical walls.

Concrete Paving

Mᴀɴᴜꜰᴀᴄᴛᴜʀᴇᴅ ᴄᴏɴᴄʀᴇᴛᴇ ᴘᴀᴠᴇʀs are extremely durable and replicate the look of natural stone (or brick) but are more regular in size and shape and less expensive. They can be laid randomly or in patterns similar to brick patterns. Some manufacturers offer concrete pavers with interlocking shapes.

Concrete can also be poured in place within borders of stone, wood, or brick. Slab-formed concrete is quite versatile: It can be heavily textured with an aggregate of stone; it can be scored, brushed, or pigmented during installation for additional texture and color; it can be stamped with a pattern when wet to resemble paving patterns of other materials; or it can be embedded with other elements, such as small pebbles or glass, for accents.

▲ A COURTYARD OF RADIATING CONCRETE PAVERS is formed within the two wings of this grand, hillside home. Built-in brick planters define the edge of the courtyard, while offering an alluring contrast in material.

◄ AN UNEXPECTED AND PRIVATE PATIO in a small lot is a pleasant alternative to a limited lawn. Here, stone steps lead down to a sunny patio set in a parquet pattern of concrete pavers that is screened from neighbors by a substantial trellis.

TILE

◄ SANDWICHED BETWEEN the pool and the lake, this tile patio presents a serene plateau. Commercial-grade tiles are particularly durable for poolside patios that get a lot of use.

▼ UNGLAZED QUARRY TILES such as these are made specifically for outdoor use and are ideal for pool surrounds. The tiles are set on a concrete base and then mortared in place. The grid of the patio tiles here is set at an intriguing angle, and the square tiles echo the window pattern of the house.

◄A FREESTANDING PERGOLA frames the view at the end of this tiled patio, creating the effect of an open-air pavilion with classical proportions that match the house. The square terra cotta tiles are distressed, lending an antique look and feel. Unglazed tile like this needs a sealant applied annually, which repels water and will help prevent cracking in the winter.

Tile Paving

CERAMIC TILE COMES glazed or unglazed, but for patio paving you want to use unglazed tiles made specifically for outdoor use—save the colorful (and very slippery) glazed tiles for decorative accents or edging.

There are three kinds of unglazed flooring tile: quarry tile, terra cotta, and porcelain tiles. Each has its own unique personality along with advantages and disadvantages.

■ Quarry tiles have a slight texture to them, offering traction without excessive unevenness.

■ Terra cotta tiles have a nice rustic look but are porous and best used only in milder climates.

■ Porcelain tiles are fired at a high temperature, making them tough and stain-resistant.

■ Both quarry and terra cotta tiles come in natural clay colors—reds, browns, and yellows—as well as pastel hues. They often imitate the look of stone, such as limestone or slate.

■ All tiles are inherently brittle and must be laid on a thick "mud-set" mortar bed over a level slab of concrete.

■ There are a variety of sealers and "enhancers" that protect tile from moisture and stains, while enhancing the natural color of unglazed tile.

Steps and Terracing

WHETHER OUT OF STYLISTIC PREFERENCE or topographical necessity, many patios incorporate one or more terraced levels connected by steps. Steps and terracing can be effective design elements, creating a sympathetic relationship between landscape and hardscape, while also solving the problems inherent to building on a slope.

Terracing—flattening out select areas of a slope or hill—can be implemented to make pleasant, flat lawns or patios. Using multiple terraced levels also provides a way to define different zones of use on a patio, such as dining versus lounging areas. And regardless of whether steps are connecting terraced levels on a hillside or simply varied features in an outdoor space—a poolside patio and raised seating patio, for instance—they provide a functional and visually compelling transitional element.

▼NARROWING AS THEY RISE from a broad base, these three-sided, pyramid-like steps form a ceremonial entrance to this patio from the poolside and offer a choice of direction when ascending or descending.

▲ THIS LUSH GARDEN features a series of terraces connected by meandering steps and retaining walls, which accommodate the changing landscape while creating an invigorating sense of motion. The beams and built up corner posts imply the structure of a small building open on all sides.

◄ A MIXTURE OF CUT PAVERS and natural fieldstone adds texture to this cozy patio nestled between house and hillside. Beyond and around the patio are a number of different zones and levels with their own individual focal points and functions. The stone steps make for a fluid transition from one level to another and tie the various levels together.

CREATING INDIVIDUAL REGIONS on a patio using different levels and surfaces gives the sense of more space and offers numerous perspectives from varying heights. Here multilevel patios incorporate a spa, dining area, and planting beds, and lead to wooden decks at the upper regions of this rear yard.

▼LIKE A WATERFALL, these stone steps take a curvy detour as they cascade down the planted slope. For well-traveled steps, having a stone "landing pad" at the bottom preserves the lawn and prevents a mud pile when it rains.

▲CUT STONE FORMS THE STEPS that contain this brick patio, and the same stone becomes a lengthy retaining wall. Broad steps like these are good for hanging out; the width should be at least 10 in. for a tread. The patio itself has an alternating herringbone and running bond that visually breaks up the expanse into smaller areas.

TERRACING TECHNIQUES

Creating a series of level patios that terrace down a hillside is achieved by cutting and filling the grade to make flat areas linked by steps. Environmental consciousness dictates that ideally all the soil that is removed from one part of the hill for a patio is reused at another.

Cut

Fill

The dotted line shows the shape of the land prior to terracing.

▲ WHEN A HOUSE HAS ACCESS to its outdoor rooms from many different levels and the property is sloped, terracing is a good way to optimize quirky space. At this multilevel patio, the bridge offers an intriguing alternative to stairs as a way of entering the house (far right) and underscores the trail to take up the hill to another outdoor zone.

Defining Boundaries

Whether you are seeking protection and privacy or you simply want to define certain areas of your outdoor space, a wall or fence can do the trick nicely. A wall or fence can limit access, define the borders, act as a guardrail at the edge of a precipice, and add a third dimension to a patio. Boundaries come in all shapes, sizes, and materials, from natural-looking stone walls to sleek concrete parapets to metal or wooden fences.

When selecting the style and material, it's important to consider the existing architecture and landscape because a wall or fence will have a big impact on the overall image of your property. For example, a picket fence would look out of place with a very modern home, as would a solid concrete wall with an English-style cottage.

▼ REPEATING A VOCABULARY OF MATERIALS throughout a site will hold it together as one composition. In this little bit of paradise, stone walls surround the pool and branch off into the landscape to make other enclosures for plantings, seating, and a shady picnic spot. The top of the wall has 2-in.-thick slabs of slate that match the poolside patio paving.

◄ LATTICE MAKES AN INEXPENSIVE way to quickly screen out unwanted views or create a sense of privacy, and it is light-weight and easily maneuverable. In this urban setting, a lattice fence separates the patio from the back alley, providing protection and privacy, as well as a support for lush plantings that transform what might have been a hot, unpleasant court into a cool oasis.

▲ THE PICKET FENCE has its origins in early American settlements, where the pickets helped reduce erosion and drifting sand around Cape Cod homes; these days it connotes a cottage-like atmosphere, as seen here. Pickets can have plain, pointed, or decoratively shaped tops, and 8-ft.-long units can be purchased at home centers for quicker installation.

WALLS

▲ IN KEEPING WITH the informality of the mortarless patio, this stone wall was dry-stacked and forms a low boundary that encircles an outdoor dining area. A wide stone wall like this needs to extend below ground level at least 2 ft. to help it resist movement as the ground freezes (contracts) and thaws (expands).

▶ A BRICK WALL OFFERS both privacy and the perfect backdrop for a trellis and colorful plantings in this suburban garden. Although picturesque, it's important to keep in mind that the vines can destroy the mortar between bricks, which may have to be replaced over time.

Stone Walls

STONE WALLS LEND PERMANENCE to a patio area, implying that some of the landscape has been "tamed" and separated from its wilder surroundings. Stone walls can be rustic or more refined, depending on the type of stone used and how it's constructed.

Dry- or wet-stacked are the most basic types of stone walls. Dry-stacked walls are formed with stones that are merely fitted together without benefit of concrete or mortar and have the most natural feel. Wet-stacked walls have mortar holding the stones together. Each can be made out of either naturally shaped stones or "dressed" stones that have been altered to present a more regular, flat face.

The look of a stone wall can also be created by veneering stone to the face of a concrete-block wall. Another option for turning a concrete or concrete-block wall into a stone wall look-alike is to use manufactured stone, which is made from concrete and formed to resemble stone.

▲ THIS "PATIO" IS DEFINED SOLELY BY the surrounding stone sea wall, which protects the seating from the salt spray. Very large stones were needed to survive the harsh winds and water in this magnificent but exposed spot; smaller stones would require more mortar or concrete, which wears away quickly in this type of environment.

▶ A DRY-STACKED FIELDSTONE WALL forms the border of this natural-looking patio. The nubby texture of the stone complements the textural qualities of the irregular fieldstone paving. This wall is brand new, but as it ages, mosses and other plants will find their way into the cracks and crevices, giving it a charming patina.

▼ TUCKING A PATIO INTO THE GROUND and surrounding it with hedges shelters it from prevailing winds. Here, a sturdy stone retaining wall is the boundary of a sunken garden terrace that makes a verdant and cozy spot for outdoor dining.

▲STONE WALLS HAVE THREE surfaces to consider—the two sides and the top. Unlike many fences, there is no unfinished or "bad" side. This low fieldstone wall looks equally appealing from patio and shore. Along with protecting people from tumbling off the edge of the raised patio, the wall provides secondary seating.

◄WHEN USING CONCRETE, it's just as easy to lay a curved wall as a straight one, so why not choose an interesting shape? This painted concrete retaining wall has lighting integrated into it, making this patio prime territory for evening entertaining. The smooth top of the wall, called a coping, should be slightly sloped to allow rainwater to run off.

▲THIS WALL OF DRESSED STONES offers a stylized solution for edging a raised patio. The steps and gates create a formal procession through multiple spaces, drawing the eye back into the property toward the house and generating a sense of welcome.

▶INTERSPERSING SMOOTH STUCCO WALLS and dressed stone walls adds visual interest to this home. Stone piers at the corners and midpoints of the stucco walls lend continuity to the whole and also hold railings that satisfy the building code.

◄ DECIDING HOW TO allocate your budget is important when patio planning. At this coastal home with a breathtaking view, the owners decided that the best way to achieve the look they wanted was to devote most of their resources to the artisan-built stone wall and use inexpensive gravel for the patio paving material.

STONE WALL STYLES

There are as many stone wall styles as there are masons, who leave their artistry in the laying of each stone.

Dressed stone laid in irregular courses

Random-coursed rubble

Fieldstone wall

FENCES AND GATES

▲ A RUSTIC FENCE made of large tree limbs looks as if it grew in place to protect the edge of this patio, which is located at the top of a steep embankment. This type of fence is a low-cost solution that just requires some ingenuity in the installation, and its naturally rounded shape sheds water.

▶ A GARDEN GATE FRAMES THE VIEW and ushers you into this gravel and paved patio with its gorgeous overlook of the water. The lattice on the side of the gate is hung vertically, rather than on a 45-degree angle, a departure from the expected. Even in the cooler months when the branches and vines are bare, there is enough detail in the lattice to retain privacy.

◄ COMPOSED OF CLOSELY SPACED metal rods supported by cedar posts, this fence creates a unique, ever-shifting shadow pattern on the adjacent paved area. Climbing roses will soon cover the fence, which won't rot or need painting as a wooden fence would.

► THIS NOT-SO-SECRET GARDEN patio sits at the end of a gravel path connected by an arched trellis accented with roses. The swinging gate has spring hinges to ensure it stays closed, better containing pets and young children. As it wraps around the large patio area, the decorative fence reverts to a simple post-and-rail construction where it is obscured within the hedges.

► THERE IS NO LIMIT TO THE SHAPE and form that gates and fences can take. This brick arch and wooden gate combo creates a solid feel without being too visually heavy in the landscape. And in this outdoor room that is part patio and part garden, the structure suggests an architectural ruin that was rediscovered and put back to use.

▲ THIS GEOMETRIC FENCE features a high-contrast pairing of solid door with transparent fence. The fence sections are filled in with a wire mesh panel that adds strength while admitting a view to the garden beyond. Posts that hold gate hinges need to be solidly anchored to withstand repetitive swinging, especially when the gate is as big as a door like this one.

Gateways

THE GARDEN GATE IS THE PORTAL that invites friends in and keeps strangers out. When a gate is part of a surrounding fence, it usually takes the same form as a section of the fence—a picket fence takes a picketed gate, and so forth. When a garden gate is at an opening in a hedge or a stone wall, it can take any form, provided the tone of the material complements the surroundings.

Since there is no supporting frame as there would be on a door, the hinge side of a gate has to be extra-strong to resist the force and carry the weight of the gate—some gates are so wide and heavy that they actually traverse on a small wheel at the bottom.

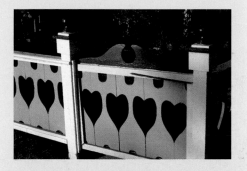

THIS CHARMING GATE INVITES rather than deters. The gate posts mark the entrance with turned finials, and a splash of red paint has been used to define the gate from the rest of the matching fence.

◀ THIS HILLSIDE PATIO RETREAT is bounded by hedges and a fence that complement the home's architecture. The fence posts are embellished with decorative finials, and the pickets—simple 1x4 boards—alternate in height.

△ WOODEN GATES ARE SUSCEPTIBLE to the weather, so they should be designed to resist warping and to limit the amount of water or snow that gathers beneath them. Cedar, which is naturally rot- and warp-resistant, was used for this gate as well as for the pergola.

▶ METAL RAILINGS ARE another option for fencing in a patio. As seen here, they can be secured directly into a stone patio with special fittings. On a straight run like this, the top ends have to be attached to something for stability.

◄ A GATE CAN BE MORE than just a flat, swinging panel in a fence. This one is a whimsical signature that sets the stage for what lies within, framing and emphasizing the view of the house beyond.

▲ EVEN IN A TIGHT LOT with close neighbors, privacy can be achieved with style. The arched beams of this arbor and the adjoining fence form a protective arcade that stretches from the street to the home's rear patio. Belgian block forms the path beneath the arbor and also edges the steps around the flagstone patio.

Overhead Structures

WHILE SUNLIGHT IS GENERALLY WELCOMED on a patio, incorporating an overhead structure to provide shelter and shade can make the space more comfortable and useful. A pergola or arbor can balance sun and shade via the direction and spacing of the joists or rafters, which work almost like the slats of a venetian blind, blocking and permitting light as the sun moves through the sky.

Another common overhead structure, a breezeway, is an extension of a house's roof that covers a portion of a patio and has open sides. A breezeway may link two wings of a house, or link the house to an outbuilding such as a garage. Some breezeways are used purely for sheltered circulation; others may be destinations complete with furniture.

▼ALTHOUGH IT HAS NO REAL WALLS OR CEILING, the architecture of this palatial pergola suggests a room, with the gesture of walls and ceiling in the border of columns and regimented rafters.

▲ A FREESTANDING CANOPY like this is a useful and inexpensive embellishment and adds a festive air. It has all the benefits of a gazebo but can be disassembled at the end of the season. Light colors let the sunlight glow through while providing some shelter from the elements.

▲ A CAPTIVATING STUDY in contrasting materials and textures, this breezeway is composed of random-sized flagstones that create a monolithic pathway under a massive wooden roof. A breezeway is a transition space; here it accentuates the passage to and from the house and serves as the dividing line between the raked gravel court (left) and the lawn.

▲ OVERHEAD LATTICE TRANSOMS between posts make this L-shaped pergola more rigid and stable, while providing a bit more privacy from the neighbors. The lattice mirrors the fence at the border of the property—a nice touch that pulls together the different elements of this sandstone patio.

▶ PERGOLAS CAN ACCENTUATE a home's architecture, in this case a cottage style with a gravel dooryard. The curved ends of the rafters that extend over the supporting beam are called rafter tails and are often decoratively cut in a swoop or other shape. Here, the curvy shapes indicate the hand of an artisan rather than a machine-made part.

THIS AIRY PERGOLA provides an inviting combination of sun and shade, and creates shadow lines that cut the glare down by half. The overhead rafters are notched to fit snugly over the supporting beams so the rafters remain true to line.

WRAPPING THE CORNER and providing a shelter, this substantial pergola forms an arcade of scented vines, giving it the feeling of a porch. In the winter when the leaves are gone, the sun can penetrate the lower windows. To ensure adequate support, it's important to consider the weight of massive vines like these when choosing framing members.

▶IN THIS UNIQUE OPEN-AIR ROOM defined by a floor and the suggestion of an exterior wall, the sky is the ceiling and the view fills in the windows and doorways created by the architecture. Over the course of the day, the planes of the wall cast ever-changing shadows that further enhance this unusual patio space.

◀MAKING GOOD USE of a seldom-visited corner of a yard, lattice-work panels frame the sitting area beneath this arbor. It relies on a triangular support system of three fence posts. Although the lattice seen here is wood, it's also available in vinyl, which requires essentially no upkeep.

Patio Maintenance

ALTHOUGH MINIMAL MAINTENANCE is necessary for patios, there are a few important housekeeping maneuvers for keeping your favorite outdoor escape functional and beautiful. Sweeping the surface clear of leaves and debris prevents organic material from rotting and potentially damaging the surface.

A patio formed of units set in sand or dirt should be inspected yearly to make sure that loose stones or bricks are reset and tamped down. Rain will provide a good wash now and then, but an occasional scrub down will prevent mold and grime from building up. And if the patio is shaded, check that there isn't too much slippery moss forming on the stones.

▲ ▶ IN THIS IMAGINATIVE ENTRY, the overhead rafters are spanned by pipes that serve as an armature for climbing plants. Instead of classical round columns, the pergola is supported by posts designed with arching brackets to resemble trees. The addition of color adds to the decorative nature of this assemblage. A bench is tucked under a roof that extends over one bay of the pergola rafters, providing a refuge in a rain shower or a special getaway place.

▲ SURROUNDED BY A LOW rock wall, a brick patio topped by a pergola of red cedar adds another outdoor room to this house. The low-maintenance combination is ideal—the cedar needs no paint, is rot-resistant, and will weather naturally; the patio and wall need only an occasional hosing off.

▶ THESE PERGOLA RAFTERS were notched at intervals to accept square purlins (smaller wood pieces) that lay perpendicular to them, adding another layer of detail. The thin purlins also contrast the sturdy supporting posts. Posts such as these are often constructed out of pressure-treated lumber, which can't be painted, and then encased in cedar to beef them up and ready them for paint.

◀ THE LAYERING OF outdoor spaces can set up a variety of experiences and activities, and this property is graced by a series of outdoor rooms that do just that. A deck (at left) just outside the door steps down to a brick patio, part of which contains an arbor that's used as a dining area. In the background is a more open-air patio area, and in the foreground the lawn offers yet another dimension for outside relaxation.

Patio Doors

To GET THE MOST USE OUT OF A PATIO, you want immediate access from your house to your outdoor room. There are several kinds of patio doors, and you should make your selection based on the architectural style of the house and the level of openness desired. Double-wide sliding doors allow only one door to be open at a time; some patio doors pivot in the center at the bottom, rotating a full 90 degrees; and with French doors, both panels are hinged to open. French doors usually open into a room but can also swing out onto a protected patio. There's also a new incarnation of French doors that slide, which eliminates the need to allow room for the door to swing in.

Sliding patio doors

Center pivot door

In-swinging French doors

Sliding French doors

▶ THIS INGENIOUS STRUCTURE creates a high-tech solution to dealing with the sun/shade dilemma at different times of the day. The segmented roof has a remote-control feature that can change these "outdoor blinds" from being open, to partially angled louvers, to a closed, watertight surface.

▶ GARDENS AND PATIOS are often intertwined, but this pergola architecturally unites the two. Situated on a very gradual hill, the pergola's beams are arranged to step up, accommodating the grade change as the slope rises toward the house.

▲ THE MASSIVE TIMBERS that make up this arbor aren't delicate, but they suit the style of this thick-walled, straw-bale house in Santa Fe and create a sturdy framework for the climbing grape and wisteria vines.

◄ WHEN YOU WANT TO ENLARGE an existing patio but don't have exact matching materials available, a sharp contrast can be the way to go, as witnessed by the patchwork of brick, stone, and wood used to good effect here. Radiating rafters arrayed on a semicircle of posts formed the soaring basket-like arbor, which echoes the curve of the stone wall.

BREEZEWAYS

▲ THIS BREEZEWAY FORMALLY CONNECTS two wings of
the house, framing the view across the pool in the
process. During rain showers, the chairs can be pulled
under the breezeway and the view still enjoyed.

▶ ACTING AS THE GATEHOUSE to a waterside patio, this
breezeway creates a picturesque intersection of two
circulation paths, one indoors and the other outside.
The doors can be shut at night or during bad weather,
transforming the breezeway into a regular hallway.

▲ SET UP AS A COMPLETE OUTDOOR ROOM, this breezeway's high ceiling permits the afternoon sun and breezes to reach, while protecting loungers from the intensity of the sun at midday.

◀ THE ANGLED SHAPE of this breezeway reconciles the offset of the two buildings and offers a covered passage between the house and garage doorways. Although the roof looks flat, it is pitched to the gutters on either side, sending the water down through concealed downspouts. The patio is a collage of Belgian block and bluestone pavers.

Poolside Patios

POOLS AND SPAS NEED SOME TYPE OF HARDSCAPING around them to anchor them and provide a transition to the surrounding landscape. While sometimes a deck, this element is often a patio devised of stone, concrete, or brick because these materials stand up to chlorinated water better than wood does. Designing a poolside patio should be approached in generally the same way as for any other type of patio; materials and style should reflect the nature and shape of the pool, while taking into consideration the landscape, house, and property as a whole. However, because bare feet and wet surfaces can make for slippery conditions, using a material that provides adequate traction is of particular concern with a poolside patio.

▼LARGE BOULDERS STREWN ALONG the edge of this pool give it a very natural effect, much like a quarry or lagoon. The large, flat stones that jut out over the pool edge make natural diving platforms or sunning rocks. Boulders with rounded, weathered edges should be used since they're more gentle on feet.

▲THIS FAIRY-TALE HOUSE has an equally enchanting pool area, creating a unified impression in the landscape. The free-form pool is surrounded by a narrow patio that follows suit; its narrow width contributes to the natural feel of the pool, allowing the rim of planting beds to have equal visual weight. The stone edging has a slightly overhanging lip that suggests a woodland pond within a grove.

▶THIS TROPICAL POOL AND PATIO PARADISE looks like an exclusive island resort, but it's actually a residence. Palm trees punctuate the edges of the patio in planters that form part of the pool edge, adding drama and visual interest.

▼ ▶ THE UNUSUAL ARCHITECTURE of this house—arcing walls, oddly angled roofs, and a collection of connecting pavilions—is echoed in the patio, where a wide arcing section faces the water. The extensive pool has both a large swimming area and a lap pool.

▲ THIS BUCOLIC POOL PATIO is part of an old farm compound and was laid with local stone. The lack of evident poolside edging gives it a natural feel despite its geometric shape. If a pool is unheated, it can be sited to receive maximum solar gain, but a shady area nearby, such as the cool grassy spot under this arbor, will make the area most comfortable.

◄ THE CURVING LINES of this patio accommodate planting beds and lend an organic feel that flows with the landscape. The wooded setting takes on a magical feel at dusk with lighting scattered around and in the pool. Lighting should be selected to set the mood.

Pool Planning

A POOL IS A HANDSOME AMENITY for any property, but it also requires a lot of resources and should be carefully planned in terms of siting, size, and safety. Here are some basic considerations:

■ Put a pool where it can gain the maximum sun exposure, which will help heat it. Also consider locating it near the door that bathers will use the most.

■ Pools are governed by building codes, which should be carefully reviewed and considered during planning. In most locales, for instance, a protective fence is required to guard against unsupervised children wandering in.

■ If you live in a northern climate, consider how many months a year you can reasonably use a pool before you install one that fills the yard.

■ A beautifully designed pool can also be enjoyed out of season if it is designed to be more than just a water-filled hole in the ground. A surrounding patio, plantings, attractive lighting, and furnishings will contribute to the poolside being a destination in your yard, even when it is too cool for a swim.

▶ THIS STRIKING POOL and patio feature an "infinite edge," meaning it appears that the water flows into the sea beyond. It really flows into a trough at the end of the pool, where it's recirculated. The bluestone patio rests tightly against the surrounding grade, so it blends into the landscape.

▲ CUT GRANITE PAVERS make a sleek and indestructible material for this modern poolside patio; they come in thick slabs that are set over a concrete bed and mortared in place. Granite can endure a wide range of temperatures and weather conditions without cracking or splitting.

◀ A PATIO NEED NOT BE LARGE to be beautiful and useful. Even though this poolside area is compact, there's enough room for a seating area, and it's made to feel cozy rather than claustrophobic with the help of smart landscaping that features a good mix of trees, plants, and flowers. The overhanging roof of the pool house offers a sheltered area.

Spas and Hot Tubs

A SPA IS A SMALL POOL that offers an extra feature or two: It could have whirlpool jets that create a refreshing turbulence; it could have a waterfall that cascades into the swimming pool; or it could offer underwater jets to massage backs and legs.

A hot tub is a spa that holds super-heated water and can also have whirlpool features so you can bubble the time away. Hot tubs and swimming pools can be adjacent, but the waters are such different temperatures that they shouldn't intermingle.

▶ IN THIS TRANQUIL SPOT, the spa is framed with slabs of bluestone, while the surrounding patio has pavers set on a diagonal, signaling a subtle pattern change. When the water is still, it becomes a reflecting pool that mirrors the tree branches.

◀ THE POSITION OF this unusually shaped pool relative to the rock garden and the gentle slope gives it the look of a miniature glacial lake. When these young trees mature, they will provide natural privacy and a windscreen.

Patio Accessories

PATIOS BECOME MUCH MORE INVITING and useful when embellished with accessories. These elements can be permanent features, such as a fireplace, or provisional additions, such as lounge chairs. Regardless, accessorizing a patio accomplishes a variety of aesthetic and functional goals.

Accessories provide a sense of scale, creating a focal point and the perception of defined space in a larger patio area and surrounding landscape. They can also provide pleasing sensory experiences, such as the sound of water bubbling in a fountain or the warmth and smell of a fire. Depending on the extent and capabilities of the feature, it can be highly functional too, from a fire pit for roasting marshmallows to a fully operational outdoor kitchen. But even small additions can have a big impact on practical use; a simple table and chairs transform a patio from an open slab into a dining nook or party room.

▼ON THIS PATIO, THE GRILL IS KING. Setting the gas grill into the massive fireplace solves the problem of smoke getting in your eyes when the wind blows, and built-in stone ledges at either side serve as useful counter space.

▲ THIS GARDEN PATIO EVOKES an Oriental carpet with its juxtaposition of colors and textures. The lily pool provides a contemplative focal point for the seating area and forms the center of a double-sided promenade through this lush landscape. In nonchlorinated water features like this one, a circulator should be used to prevent stagnancy.

◄ ENTWINED WITH CLEMATIS VINES, this patio seat, which is built into the arbor, creates a cozy nook in a larger patio space. For outdoor furnishings made of wood, a full-bodied stain or whitewash will hold up better than paint because it simply fades rather than peels.

FIRE ELEMENTS

▶ A MONUMENTAL FIREPLACE like this can generate enough heat for the patio to be enjoyed nearly year-round. It must be vented up through a flue that is tied in to a chimney at the house. In keeping with its rough-hewn look, sections of tree trunks serve as stools to perch on while toasting marshmallows. The metal rod at the front of the fireplace is used as a rotisserie.

▲ A PATIO FIREPLACE can be a welcoming beacon on chilly nights. This one shares a chimney with an indoor counterpart, negating the need for a separate ventilation system. The tile fireplace surround imparts an exotic elegance to the stucco façade while framing the warm blaze within.

Outdoor Fireplaces

THERE ARE FEW PLEASURES more primal than sitting at an open flame. While the ever-present gas grill is good for cooking, it's not something to sit and swap ghost stories around. For a more atmospheric option, try a fire pit, a freestanding stone fireplace, a chiminea, or an old-fashioned brick barbecue. With any of these, common sense rules: Locate them on a noncombustible surface well away from the house or any other combustible materials. Be aware that wind can carry sparks or embers, and never leave a fire alone.

▲ HERE THE PATIO TAKES THE SHAPE of the wall of the house, as if it had fallen away to reveal the insides of the home. The chimney creates the only solid part of the glass wall, blurring the perception of indoors and out, and acting as the transitional element between the two.

◄ THIS STRIKING, DRESSED FIELD-STONE FIREPLACE is raised to align with the stone wall surrounding the patio, bringing the fire closer to eye level.

▶ THE MASONRY PATIO around this massive chimney/fireplace does double duty as its extended hearthstone. A chimney this hefty needs height to achieve a balanced look and feel. The patio is attached to a wooden deck that further extends the foot-print of the house with several outdoor rooms.

Outdoor Kitchens

IN SOUTHERN CLIMES, the outdoor "summer kitchen" was the norm, allowing cooking to be done without heating up the house. Today's outdoor kitchen is more about adding to our enjoyment of the outdoors and sharing a meal with friends.

In addition to your typical kitchen appliances—sink, stove, fridge—also consider a built-in gas grill, a bar-sized sink, ice maker, and other kitchen conveniences.

There are a couple of practical matters when installing outdoor kitchens: Ensure that water can be shut off at the source in cold weather so pipes won't freeze; decide whether you want to run a gas line from the house or use propane tanks; and provide an electrical source.

▲ HAVING A FULLY OPERATIONAL KITCHEN for patio parties saves a lot of back-and-forth by the hosts, and this outdoor kitchen features running water, refrigerator, and dishes too.

▲ THIS MULTILEVEL DECK AND PATIO combination allows for a handsome redwood built-in kitchen with all the amenities: grill, sink, tile countertop, electrical outlets, and storage space for a gas tank and other equipment.

◄ FOR THOSE WHO ARE SERIOUS about outdoor dining, a portable gas grill just won't do. This concrete patio boasts its own built-in gas stove flanked by prep and serving counters so you never have to leave your guests during a cookout.

WATER ELEMENTS

▶ IN THIS MAN-MADE LAGOON off the ocean, a floating, tiled patio island is reached by a bridge spanning the pool, creating a destination with a totally tropical ambience. The round shape of the island is mirrored by the thatched umbrella overhead.

▼ WATER FEATURES PROMINENTLY on this patio situated away from the house. Slabs of limestone reach out to form a path that directs movement into the hot tub area. Because of the irregular paving configuration, quirky planting beds will grow to form a privacy screen for the hot tub and outdoor shower.

▼WATER FEATURES CAN BE solely practical, too. This outdoor shower makes a handy addition to any home near a beach, as this one is, but it's also useful for dog washing and bucket filling. A privacy fence isn't necessary in a rural location like this, although it would be a design consideration in areas with neighbors.

▲THIS STUNNING VEST-POCKET LIMESTONE PATIO extends the view from the house , as well as its footprint. The fountain turns a blank wall into a provocative focal point, and its meditative gurgling floats inside, connecting indoors and out through sound.

▶STRIPES OF GRANITE BLOCK radiate out from this tiered fountain's brick backdrop, forming a visually serene center for the patio. This unique structure also incorporates a planter, and the circular, built-in flagstone seat adds a practical touch.

FURNISHINGS

▶THIS GENEROUSLY SIZED CANVAS UMBRELLA is broad enough to cover all the folks seated around the table. Umbrellas come in various fabrics, from canvas to vinyl to nylon; regardless of material, they should be allowed to dry out before they are furled, to avoid mildew.

▼THESE RUGGED BENCHES are made of durable materials, usually teak, which lasts a long time even when subjected to the elements. If resources allow, it's worth it to purchase heavy-duty, top-of-the-line outdoor furniture because the materials and fasteners used for assembly are of better quality than less expensive furniture.

▶EVEN A PLAIN CONCRETE PATIO can be beautified with the addition of elegant plantings and whimsical decor. Keep comfort in mind as well, and consider adequate cushions for the seating. Scents can be as important as views on the patio, and here wisteria peeks through the fence to entice the eyes and nose.

▲ THIS BENCH AND ACCOMPANYING
BIRDBATH turn a lush spot into a
usable oasis, complete with a
stunning view of a valley below.
Cast-concrete or stone benches
like this are heavy to shift around
and some are actually fastened to
the ground with a steel anchor to
prevent them from being tipped
over, so choose their placement
wisely.

◄ THE ARBOR ON THIS VERDANT
BRICK PATIO is substantial enough
to support a sturdy swing, offering the perfect spot to read or
relax. The swing needs to be set
at the same height as a stationary
bench would be (15 in. to 18 in.
from the floor), so you can use
your feet to keep things moving.

Breaking Away

NOT ALL OUTDOOR ROOMS HAVE TO ADJOIN THE HOUSE—sometimes it's preferable to be surrounded by the landscape instead of planted right outside the back door. The usable area of a property can be extended when there are outdoor spaces separate from the house; these may be the primary outdoor rooms or they may be alluring alternatives to an existing deck or patio.

Many people find relaxing refuge strolling along a meandering path or spending time in little outbuildings, such as gazebos or cabanas, or in other destinations on the property, such as summer houses or meditation gardens.

The limitations and assets of your site can suggest the best spot for an outdoor room. For example, if there is not a sunny area that works for a deck or patio right up against the house, then consider locating the space, whether it's a path, outbuilding, or garden area, where it will take advantage of good light, a special view, or even a more level area. Let your site and imagination be your guides.

◄ SERVING AS A PAVED INTERMEDIARY between the manicured lawn and the more natural and exotic landscaping to the side, this walkway contains a number of straight sections that take 90-degree turns, setting up a visually appealing geometric pattern in the garden.

Walkways and Paths

ONNECTING A HOUSE TO OUTDOOR ROOMS, and the outdoor rooms to each other, walkways and paths take us to the far reaches of the property and back again—from the street or driveway around back to the deck, or from a patio through the garden or down to the water's edge. The most direct route isn't necessarily the most interesting, so there's a lot of leeway to use your imagination and creativity to design your property's pathways.

Materials for walkways and paths are generally the same as those for patios (although boardwalks are worth entertaining as well), and the same installation techniques are used: The pavers are either bedded in sand or laid upon a concrete slab. Material selection should be approached the same way as it would for a patio; consider budget, style, landscaping, and how the overall design will complement its surroundings.

▲TRAVERSING A SLOPE LIKE THIS is easy when you are moving along the width of it; this plan allows the walkway to stay relatively flat. Runoff from the hillside is slowed by the ground cover and plantings. Low landscape lights illuminate the path at dusk, providing comfort.

◄LARGE STONES WITH UNEVEN bottoms, such as these, need to be set carefully so that they don't rock—digging a hole a few inches deeper and pouring a bit of concrete will help anchor them during many seasons of freezing and thawing of the earth. This path, made of naturally shaped fieldstone pavers laid on a wider gravel trail, gives the impression of stepping stones following the path of a gravel "river."

◄ ONE APPROACH TO LAYING rectangular pavers is to vary the alignment so that no two align along the length of the pathway. This makes the design less predictable and more artistic and eliminates the potential tripping hazard when four stones' corners meet at one point. The strong direction and texture of these pavers form a truly distinctive walkway.

▼ SQUARES ENLIVEN the rhythmic pattern of this walkway, which consists of running bond bricks with a square of concrete every eight courses. Laying the bricks at the sides of the path with their short ends sticking up holds the field bricks in place and adds another shape to the pattern.

▲ WALKWAYS CAN BE COMPOSED of mixed materials, as illustrated to good effect here, where the varied palette of brick and block has a casual, homemade quality to it. To achieve a level walking surface when mixing materials, make sure the top surfaces are flush as they're laid .

▶ FITTED TOGETHER LIKE PUZZLE PIECES, paths and patios made of random flagstones, like this one, have a spontaneous and artistic quality because their final effect is in large part dependent on the artisan selecting and laying the stone. This type of path can be expanded easily by laying additional stones.

Widths for Paths and Walkways

WIDTH IS AN IMPORTANT consideration for a path; you should consider how the path will be used and whether one or two people will be walking on it together. One person can walk easily down a stepping-stone path with stones that are a mere foot across, but for a more regular paved walkway, 2 ft. wide is the minimum for one person, especially if the path is bounded on both sides by plantings. For two to walk side by side, a walkway should be at least 42 in., and 48 in. is more comfortable if you are carrying things.

42-48 in.

PRIMARY WALKWAY
• Connects the street or driveway to primary entrances
• Firm and level underfoot
• Easily cleared of snow
• Most formal
• Two adults can walk side by side

24-36 in.

SECONDARY PATH OR WALKWAY
• Connects the house to a patio or outbuildings
• Firm and level underfoot
• For strolling among the plantings
• Less formal

12-16 in.

TERTIARY PATHWAY
• Seasonal—for warmer months
• Connects garden areas
• Uneven underfoot
• Stepping stones
• Least formal

◄WHEN PLANNING a stepping stone path such as this one, take into account the length of a typical adult stride—too long or too short is awkward, and if the stepping stones are arbitrarily placed, your foot will land in between the stones. You can lay down newspapers or cardboard to measure this out before setting the stones.

▲A WOODEN WALKWAY LIKE THIS is the way to go when dealing with access issues—you can connect to a deck right out of a back door without intermediate steps, and in wet weather you don't have to deal with mud.

▼SMALL UNITS ARE EASIER to place in a curve, as seen with this brick path laid in a basketweave pattern. The path can smoothly take a detour around obstacles, such as this stone bench, which makes an inviting place to pause. This type of path can also be shoveled easily and can be negotiated by a stroller or wheelchair.

Structures in the Landscape

WHETHER FOR A BREATH OF FRESH AIR, a shady spot for iced tea, a place to change into a bathing suit, or a romantic hideaway, there are a lot of little outbuildings that offer great places to unwind. These structures can be big or small, simple or elaborate, and can range from gazebos to pool cabanas and from meditation gardens to party pavilions.

Gazebos are probably the most common outbuildings. They can be freestanding or incorporated into a deck or patio. They are open sided with a roof and usually a floor, but this basic form is now taking many different configurations. Waterside structures come in a variety of shapes as well, encompassing everything from a whimsical tiki bar to a simple changing booth to a fully furnished pool or beach house.

Research local codes before you begin work on an outbuilding and look into the options available: There are do-it-yourself kits, preassembled units, and, of course, custom-designed structures.

▼ A SIMPLE STRUCTURE is all one needs for a quick-change cubicle or a place to store the rubber rafts and towels. This utilitarian pool house is flanked by solid fencing that conceals the pool equipment beyond.

◀ PERCHED ON A LITTLE HILL, this gazebo evokes a small-town bandstand. The steps help define it as a separate space in the larger deck area. As with decks, all of the gazebo railings have to conform to code as far as height and spacing of balusters.

▲ AN OUTDOOR SHOWER is a convenient amenity for a waterside home. In this well-contained shower/changing booth, the overlapping lattice provides just enough privacy, and a roof protects the bather from above. Consider where the soapy water runs off—a deep, gravel dry well is often enough, but you may be required to provide a drainage pipe that directs the gray water into your sewer system.

GAZEBOS AND CABANAS

▲ A GAZEBO THAT IS SET AWAY from the house can have its own style—it can look a little more fanciful or exotic and doesn't necessarily have to "match" the architecture of the house. And a gazebo doesn't have to be large to be enjoyed; this cozy one is only 10 ft. across.

◄ SOME CREATIVE THINKING resulted in this lovely structure, which combines the best qualities of gazebo, arbor, and zen garden. When the vines that are starting to climb one post make it all the way up, the roof framing will have intertwining greenery to add shade and scent. Millstones such as the one gracing the center of the gazebo have found a new purpose in contemporary gardens and yards.

Gazebos

IT'S THOUGHT THAT GAZEBOS most likely evolved from the Japanese tea house, but similar little open-air pavilions were found alongside Dutch canals and Chinese garden shelters. Usually thought of as small, freestanding, romantic structures at the far ends of lawns or gardens, gazebos are meant to be seen as well as occupied. Their decorative aspect is interpreted most often in wood, and they may take the form of a rustic shelter or an elaborately detailed affair showing off the skill of the carpenter. Gazebos are being reinterpreted and crafted out of other materials too, such as metal, stone, and even concrete. A newer iteration of the gazebo is as a corner piece integrated into a deck.

The architectural elements of a gazebo are the wall panels, roof, and floor/foundation. Gazebos are typically hexagonal or octagonal because those shapes suggest the intimacy of a circle while being easier to construct than a truly circular building. Gazebo roofs come to a point and are sometimes topped with a decorative finial or even a cupola or dovecote. Roofs can be conical, bell shaped, pagoda shaped, or faceted, and can be covered in wood or asphalt shingles, roll roofing, tile, or metal (such as copper or terne). Nearly any material can be used for a gazebo floor, but if wood is chosen, the floor should rest on a concrete or stone foundation that raises it off the ground to prevent rotting.

▲ COHESIVELY COMPOSED from top to bottom, this gazebo features floorboards laid in a concentric pattern to mirror the construction of the roof, and the decorative brackets and balustrade have the same lacy quality as the wicker chairs.

◄ LARGE GAZEBOS NEED A FIRM concrete foundation to carry the weight and connect the wood down to solid ground below the frost line—either posts resting on concrete piers or a continuous concrete foundation wall around the rim. Glowing like a Chinese lantern after dark, this gazebo sports a louvered cupola that adds visual interest day or night.

◄ PUTTING A GAZEBO IN an out-of-the-way spot in the garden produces an unexpected and pleasant destination to happen upon, and this one is tucked in to the woods. The onion-shaped dome clad in red roll roofing has the look of a Turkish mosque and is slightly faceted up to the whimsical finial on top.

▼ THE CONICAL-ROOFED GAZEBO was built on a very gentle rise—a good choice because siting a gazebo in a low-lying spot sets you up for dampness and even flooding. The screened sides are a boon during mosquito season and make this an appealing spot for a small campout.

GAZEBO STYLES

An octagonal gazebo's architectural style is expressed most strongly by the shape of its roof. The eight-faceted roof construct can have all manner of swoops and straight lines, or it can be built with a dome-shaped or conical topper. The shape of the roof indicates the historic or architectural style of the gazebo, while the details of the railings, enclosure panels, and other decorative elements further define the overall character.

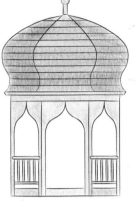

FLAT FACETS　　**BELL SHAPED**　　**PAGODA SHAPED**　　**CONICAL**　　**ONION DOME**

◄ ▲ SITTING ON A STONE BASE that roots it to the ground, a picturesque gazebo anchors the corner of an extensive deck. The space between the deck and the ground surface is vented through the lattice that wraps around it, providing both aesthetics and function. The shingled roof of the gazebo matches that of the house, tying the two together unobtrusively, and the simple design of the railing-and-post system is appropriate for such a large outdoor room.

▲ WHEN A POOL IS DISTANT from the house, it's a
great advantage to have a good-sized pool house
that can offer food, drink, and a place to change without having to trudge back and forth. Nestled into the
side of the hill, this attractive hipped-roof building is
a welcome oasis on a hot summer day.

▶ THE POOL AREA often consists of many elements—
the pool itself, a patio, and perhaps even a shade
structure—so it's important to achieve a cohesive
design. Here the cabana is attached to one end of the
pergola, and the two are integrated in several ways:
The spacing of the pergola columns is carried through
along the face of the cabana, as is the rafter-tail
design. The explicit attention to detail unifies the
parts of this poolside pavilion.

▲ ▶ OFFERING SUN WORSHIPERS a midday retreat from the sun, this special place can also be used to read in solitude, enjoy an outdoor meal, or take shelter from a thunderstorm. Although it looks like an ancient Greek temple transported to the shore, it is actually two little buildings connected by an open-air structure of lattice and roofing. Most seaside towns have strict environmental rules, so check local codes.

◀ BUILT-IN BENCHES AT EACH SIDE do double duty in this waterside arbor, providing seating as well as structural integrity and rigidity at the base of each column. The inviting structure serves as a broad gateway to the pond and a perfect getaway spot.

THE HOMEOWNERS of this "summer house" wanted an outbuilding for dining and entertaining with a view of their pond. The result is a dramatic and unique structure nestled into the landscape between the hillside and the water.

THE BUILDING was constructed of white cedar that has been left to weather naturally and blend into its surroundings. When open, the shuttered doors allow the elements in; when closed, they form a wall against inclement weather. Blurring the distinction between inside and out, trees were planted at the perimeter—as they grow, they'll turn the overhead beams into an arbor of sorts.

THE ROUND CANOPY-LIKE "ROOF" in the middle is echoed by the ring of gravel embedded in the granite flagstone terrace. The canopy is on a steel frame with a pulley system that permits it to be removed in the off-season.

◄ AT THIS SPECIAL DESTINATION, different types of stone and several unique features combine to form a serene retreat with a sculptural quality. A woodland path extends from the house down a series of stone steps to a circular meditation garden edged in native fieldstone, where a red cast-concrete water basin rests on a patio of bluestone dust.

▼ DENSE PLANTINGS can have a richer effect than spreading the same plants across a wider area, as exemplified by this enclosed garden. Traversed through unique gate posts topped with birdhouses, the path has a harlequin pattern of grass and stepping stones winding its way through the flowers, and a definite rim at the circumference defines the garden within the surrounding meadow.

Sources

Professional Organizations

The following professional organizations, trade organizations, and manufacturers offer product information, tips, and lists of members and/or contractors, installers, and suppliers for deck and patio components.

**American Institute
of Architects (AIA)**
202-898-2444
www.aiaaccess.com
Lists architects who are members of AIA. The Web site allows you to search for AIA architects in your area.

American Society of Interior Designers (ASID)
Main Web site: www.asid.org
For names of ASID members in your area, go to the referral Web site: www.interiors.org.

American Society of Landscape Architects (ASLA)
202-546-3480
www.asla.org
Web site offers tips on choosing a landscape architect and access to members.

Associated Landscape Contractors of America (ALCA)
800-395-ALCA
www.alca.org
Members are a mix of design/build contractors, installation, landscape maintenance, and interior landscape firms.

**National Association
of Home Builders (NAHB)**
800-368-5242
www.nahb.org
Includes builders and remodelers. Web site features consumer pages on planning a remodeling project and choosing a contractor.

National Association of the Remodeling Industry (NARI)
800-611-6274
www.nari.org
List of contractors.

Lumber Information

California Redwood Association (CRA)
888-225-7339
www.calredwood.org

Southern Forest Products Association (SFPA)
504-443-4464
www.sfpa.org

Western Red Cedar Lumber Association (WCRA)
604-684-0266
www.wrcla.org

Western Wood Products Association (WWPA)
503-224-3930

Synthetic Decking and Railing

Carefree U.S. Plastic Lumber/Earth Care Products
888-733-2546
www.smartdeck.com

Heritage Vinyl Products
601-726-4223
www.heritagevinyl.com

Louisiana Pacific
800-521-4316
www.weatherbest.lpcorp.com

Royal Crown, Ltd.
800-488-5245
www.royalcrownltd.com

Trex Company
800-289-8739
www.trex.com

Stone Information

National Stone, Sand, & Gravel Association
705-525-8788
www.nssga.org

Two search engines for the stone industry:
www.stoneinfo.com
www.natural-stone.com

Concrete Information

Cast Stone Institute
770-868-5909
www.caststone.org

Interlocking Concrete Pavement Institute (ICPI)
202-712-9036
www.icpi.org

Lighting

American Lighting Association
800-274-4484
www.americanlightingassoc.com

Kichler Landscape Lighting
800-875-4216
www.kichler.com

Kim Lighting
818-968-5666
www.kimlighting.com

Lighting Research Center
518-276-8716
www.lrc.rpi.edu

The Lighting Resource
952-939-1717
www.lightresource.com

Nightscaping
800-544-4840
www.nightscaping.com

World's Greatest Lighting Manufacturing List
www.lighting-inc.com

Gazebos and Garden Structures

Dalton Pavilions
215-721-1492
www.daltonpavilions.com

LMT Products
888-570-5252
www.lmtproducts.com

Vixen Hill
800-423-2766
www.vixenhill.com

Pools/Spas

National Spa & Pool Institute (NSPI)
800-323-3996
www.nspi.org

Windows/Doors

Andersen
800-426-4261
www.andersenwindows.com

Kolbe & Kolbe
800-955-8177
www.kolbe-kolbe.com

Marvin
800-241-9450
www.marvin.com

Pella
800-547-3552
www.pella.com

General Web Sites

www.taunton.com/fhb
The Web site of *Fine Homebuilding* magazine has links to a large list of information sites, manufacturers, and publications. Categories include environmentally conscious building, kit homes, kitchen and bath, and tools. This site is also a good source for product and design ideas and has access to a forum for those interested in home design.

www.build.com
This is a building and home mprovement directory that provides links to manufacturers of building products, home products, building publications, and an extensive list of builders, designers, real estate agents, and mortgage brokers.

Credits

CHAPTER 1

p. 2: (left) Photo by Charles Miller, courtesy *Fine Homebuilding,* © The Taunton Press; (spread) Photo © Brian Vanden Brink, Photographer 2003.

p. 3: (right) Photo © Robert Perron, Photographer.

p. 4: Photo © Brian Vanden Brink, Photographer 2003, Architect: Dominic Mercadante, Belfast, ME.

p. 5: Photo © davidduncanlivingston.com.

p. 6: Photo © Robert Perron, Photographer, Design: Structura, Branford, CT

p. 7: Photo © Mark Samu, Architect: Mojo Stumer, AIA, Roslyn, NY.

p. 8: Photo by David Ericson, © The Taunton Press, Inc., Architect: Patrick McClane, Richmond, VA.

p. 9: Photo © Brian Vanden Brink, Photographer 2003, Architects: Elliott & Elliott Architects, Blue Hill, ME.

p. 10: Photo © davidduncanlivingston.com.

p. 11: Photos © 2003 carolynbates.com, Design and construction: Ken Evans and Wayne Wilson, Kingsley Mill, East Clarendon, VT.

p. 12: Photo © Robert Perron, Photographer.

p. 13: (left) Photo © 2003 carolynbates.com, Architects: Cushman & Beckstrom Architecture and Planning, Inc., Stowe, Vermont; (right) Photo © Brian Vanden Brink, Photographer 2003.

p. 14: Photo © davidduncanlivingston.com.

p. 15: Photo © Mark Samu, courtesy Hearst Specials.

p. 16: Photo © 2003 carolynbates.com, Architects: Cushman & Beckstrom Architecture and Planning, Inc.

p. 17: Photo © 2003 carolynbates.com, Architect: Tom Cullins, AIA, Truex, Cullens & Partners, Burlington, VT.

CHAPTER 2

p. 18: Photo by Charles Miller, courtesy *Fine Homebuilding,* © The Taunton Press, Inc., Architect: Scott Stemper, Seattle, WA.

p. 19: Photo © Kerri Spier.

p. 20: Photo by Andy Engel, courtesy *Fine Homebuilding,* © The Taunton Press, Inc., Designer: Scott Padgett, Idyllwild, CA.

p. 21: (top) Photo © Brian Vanden Brink, Photographer 2003, Mark Hutker & Associates Architects, Vineyard Haven, MA; (bottom) Photo © Brian Vanden Brink, Photographer 2003.

p. 22: (top) Photo courtesy California Redwood Association, Design: John Hemingway, Los Altos, CA; (bottom) Photo © Robert Perron, Photographer, Robert Knight Architects, Blue Hill, ME.

p. 23: Photos © 2003 carolynbates.com, General contractor: Peter Clarke, Peter B. Clarke Contracting, Inc., Shrewsbury, VT.

p. 25: (top) Photo © Robert Perron, Photographer, Robert Knight Architects, Blue Hill, ME; (bottom) Photo © Brian Vanden Brink, Photographer 2003, Design: Heartwood Log Homes, Nova Scotia, Canada.

p. 26: (left) Photo by Charles Miller, courtesy *Fine Homebuilding,* © The Taunton Press, Inc., Architect: Keith Moskow, Boston, MA; (right) Photo © Kerri M. Spier, Designer/builder: John and Kerri Spier, Block Island, RI.

p. 27: (top) Photo © 2003 carolynbates.com, Architect: Marcel Beaudin, South Burlington, VT, Contractor: Hubbard Construction Inc., Williston, VT; (bottom) Photo © 2003 carolynbates.com.

p. 28: Photo © 2003 carolynbates.com, Architect: Malcolm Appleton, AIA, Waitsfield, VT.

p. 29: Photos © Brian Vanden Brink, Photographer 2003, Peter Bethanis, Architect, Kents Hill, ME.

p. 30: Photo © Mark Samu, courtesy Hearst Specials.

p. 31: (top left) Photo by Roe Osborn, courtesy *Fine Homebuilding,* © The Taunton Press, Inc., Architect: Laura Kraft, Seattle, WA; (right) Photo © Brian Vanden Brink, Photographer 2003, Stephen Blatt Architects, Portland, ME; (bottom left) Photo © Brian Vanden Brink, Photographer 2003.

p. 32: Photo by Roe Osborn, courtesy *Fine Homebuilding,* © The Taunton Press, Inc., Architect: Geoffrey Prentiss, San Juan Island, WA

p. 33: (top) Photo © Brian Vanden Brink, Photographer 2003; (bottom) Photo © davidduncanlivingston.com.

p. 34: (left) Photo courtesy California Redwood Association, Design: Decks by Kiefer, Pittstown, NJ; (top right) Photo © Robert Perron, Photographer, Architect: Nelson Denny, Hadlyme, CT; (bottom right) Photo © Robert Perron, Photographer, Paul Bailey, Architect, New Haven, CT

p. 35: Photo by Scott Gibson, courtesy Fine Homebuilding, © The Taunton Press, Inc.

p. 36: (top) Photo courtesy Trex Company, Inc., (bottom) Photo by Charles Miller, courtesy *Fine Homebuilding,* © The Taunton Press, Inc.

p. 37: Photo © Mark Samu.

p. 38: Photo © Jessie Walker.

p. 39: (top) Photo by Charles Miller, courtesy *Fine Homebuilding,* © The Taunton Press, Inc.; (bottom) Photo © 2003 carolynbates.com, Tim Holloway, Distinctive Restoration, Inc., Monkton, VT.

p. 40: (top) Photo © Brian Vanden Brink, Photographer 2003, Rob Whitten Architect, Portland, ME; (bottom) Photo © Robert Perron, Photographer, Robert Knight Architects, Blue Hill, ME.

p. 42: (top) Photo © 2003 carolynbates.com, Cushman + Beckstrom Architecture and Planning, Inc., Stowe, VT; (bottom) Photo © Robert Perron, Photographer, Estes & Co. Architects, Newport, RI.

p. 43: Photo © davidduncanlivingston.com.

p. 44: (top left) Photo by Roe Osborn, courtesy *Fine Homebuilding,* © The Taunton Press, Inc., Arthur Chenoweth, OR; (top right) Photo © Robert Perron, Photographer, Robert Knight Architects, Blue Hill, ME; (bottom) Photo © Brian Vanden Brink, Photographer 2003, Horiuchi & Solien Landscape Architects, Falmouth, MA.

p. 45: Photo © Robert Perron, Photographer, Architect: Straus-Edwards, Woodbury, CT.

p. 46: (top) Photo © Brian Vanden Brink, Photographer 2003, Architect: Steven Foote, Boston, MA; (bottom) Photo © Brian Vanden Brink, Photographer 2003, Jack Silverio Architects, Lincolnville, ME.

p. 47: (top) Photo © Brian Vanden Brink, Photographer 2003, Donham & Sweeney Architects, Boston, MA; (bottom) Photo courtesy *Fine Homebuilding,* © The Taunton Press, Inc.

p. 48: Photo © Jim Westphalen, Truex, Cullins & Partners Architects, Burlington, VT.

p. 49: (top right) Photo © davidduncanlivingston.com; (top left) Photo © Mark Samu, Architect: Austen Patterson Diston, AIA, Southport, CT; (bottom) Photo © Brian Vanden Brink, Photographer 2003, Elliott & El-

liott Architects, Blue Hill, ME.

p. 50: (top) Photo © Robert Perron, Photographer, Architect: Tony Terry, Branford, CT; (bottom) Photo © Robert Perron, Photographer, Noyes Vogt Architects, Guilford, CT.

p. 51: Photo © Mark Samu, courtesy Hearst Specials.

p. 52: (top) Photo by Jeff Beneke, © The Taunton Press, Inc.; (bottom) Photo © Brian Vanden Brink, Photographer 2003, Architect: Jack Silverio, Lincolnville, ME.

p. 53: (top) Photo by Jeff Beneke, © The Taunton Press, Inc.; (bottom) Photo © 2003 carolynbates.com, Architect: Marcel Beaudin, South Burlington, VT, General contractor: George Hubbard, Hubbard Construction, Inc., Williston, VT.

p. 54: Photo © Brian Vanden Brink, Photographer 2003, Margo Jones, Architect, Greenfield, MA.

p. 55: (top) Photo © Brian Vanden Brink, Photographer 2003, Tony DiGregorio Architect, Damariscotta, ME; (bottom) Photo © Robert Perron, Photographer, Elena Kalman, Architect, Stamford, CT.

p. 56: (top) Photo courtesy California Redwood Association; (bottom) Photo © 2003 carolynbates.com, Jean Henshaw Design, Shelburne, VT.

p. 57: (top) Photo © Robert Perron, Photographer, Robert Knight Architects, Blue Hill, ME; (bottom) Photo by Roe Osborn, courtesy Fine Homebuilding, © The Taunton Press, Inc., Architect: Bryan Wilson, Block Island, RI.

p. 58: (top) Photo © Robert Perron, Photographer, Interior Design, Old Lyme, CT; (bottom) Photo © Robert Perron, Photographer.

p. 59: (top) Photo © Ken Gutmaker; (bottom) Photo by Charles Miller, courtesy *Fine Homebuilding,* © The Taunton Press, Inc.

p. 60: (top) Photo © Robert Perron, Photographer, Robert Knight Architects, Blue Hill, ME; (bottom) Photo © 2003 carolynbates.com, Architect: Michael Wisniewski, Duncan-Wisniewski Architects, Burlington, VT.

p. 61: (top) Photo © 2003 carolynbates.com, Architect: Malcolm Appleton, AIA, Waitsfield, VT; (bottom) Photo © Robert Perron, Photographer.

p. 62: Photo © Robert Perron, Photographer, Paul Bailey Architect, New Haven, CT.

p. 63: (top) Photo © 2003 carolynbates.com, Cushman & Beckstrom Architecture and Planning, Inc., Stowe, VT; (bottom) Photo by Charles Bickford, courtesy *Fine Homebuilding,* © The Taunton Press, Inc., Architect: Charles Mueller, Centerbrook Architects, Essex, CT.

p. 64: Photo © 2003 carolynbates.com, Office of H. Keith Wagner, Landscape Architects, Burlington, VT.

p. 65: (top left) Photo © Brian Vanden Brink, Photographer 2003, Mark Hutker & Associates Architects, Vineyard Haven, MA; (right) Photo © Robert Perron, Photographer, Robert Knight Architects, Blue Hill, ME; (bottom left) Photo © Robert Perron, Photographer, Architect: J. P. Franzen, Southport, CT; Oliver Nurseries, Fairfield, CT.

p. 66: (top) Photo © Jessie Walker; (bottom) Photo © Robert Perron, Photographer, Architect: William Nowysz, Iowa City, IA.

p. 68: (top) Photo © Robert Perron, Photographer, JP Franzer Architects, Guilford, CT; (bottom) Photo © Ken Gutmaker.

p. 69: Photo © Robert Perron, Photographer.

p. 70: (top) Photo © Brian Vanden Brink, Pho-

tographer 2003, Winton Scott Architects, Portland, ME; (bottom) Photo © Robert Perron, Photographer, B&B Landscaping, Mystic, CT.

p. 71: (top) Photo © Brian Vanden Brink, Photographer 2003, Architect: Jack Silverio, Lincolnville, ME; (bottom) Photo © Robert Perron, Photographer, Ken Walden Landscape, ME.

p. 72: Photo © Robert Perron, Photographer, Landscape: John Wanerka, Branford, CT.

p. 73: (top) Photo © davidduncanlivingston.com; (bottom) Photo © Brian Vanden Brink, Photographer 2003.

p. 74: (top) Photo © 2003 carolynbates.com, Cushman & Beckstrom Architecture and Planning, Inc., Stowe, VT; (bottom) Photo © Brian Vanden Brink, Photographer 2003, Mark Hutker & Associates Architects, Vineyard Haven, MA.

p. 75: Photo © Brian Vanden Brink, Photographer 2003, Heartland Log Homes, Nova Scotia, Canada.

p. 76: Photo © Brian Vanden Brink, Photographer 2003, Bernhard & Priestly Architects, Rockport, ME.

p. 77: (top) Photo © Brian Vanden Brink, Photographer 2003; (bottom Photo © Robert Perron, Photographer, Nelson Denny Architects, Hadlyme, CT.

p. 78: Photo © davidduncanlivingston.com.

p. 79: Photo © Mark Samu, John Hummel Construction.

p. 80: Photos © Robert Perron, Photographer, Robert Knight Architects, Blue Hill, ME.

p. 81: (top) Photo © Robert Perron, Photographer, Noyes/Vogt Architects, Guilford, CT; (bottom) Photo © Jessie Walker.

CHAPTER 3

p. 82: Photo by Charles Miller, courtesy Fine Homebuilding, © The Taunton Press, Inc., House + House Architects, San Francisco.

p. 83: Photo © Robert Perron, Photographer.

p. 84: Photo © Brian Vanden Brink, Photographer 2003, Architect: Jack Silverio, Lincolnville, ME.

p. 85: (top) Photo © 2003 carolynbates.com, Design: Linda Vail, ASID, Vail Design Group, Colchester, VT (bottom) Photo © Brian Vanden Brink, Photographer 2003.

p. 86: Photo © Robert Perron, Photographer, Zak Landscape, CT.

p. 87: (top) Photo © Brian Vanden Brink, Photographer 2003, Architect: Peter Rose, Cambridge, MA; (bottom) Photo © 2003 carolynbates.com, Cushman & Beckstrom Architecture and Planning, Inc.

p. 88: (top) Photo by Charles Miller, courtesy Fine Homebuilding, © The Taunton Press, Inc., House + House Architects, San Francisco, CA; (bottom) Photo by Andy Engel, courtesy *Fine Homebuilding,* © The Taunton Press, Inc., Architect: Kevin McKenna, Columbia, MD.

p. 89: (top) Photo © Brian Vanden Brink, Photographer 2003, Architect: Lo Yi Chan, New York, NY; (bottom) Photo © Robert Perron, Photographer, Architect: Kagan Company, New Haven, CT.

p. 90: Photo © Brian Vanden Brink, Photographer 2003, Ron Forest Fences, Scarborough, ME.

p. 91: (top) Photo © Brian Vanden Brink, Photographer 2003, Mark Hutker & Associates, Architects, Vineyard Haven, MA (bottom) Photo © Brian Vanden Brink, Photographer 2003, Horiuchi & Solien Landscape Architects, Falmouth, MA.

p. 92: (left) Photo © Todd Caverly/Brian Vanden Brink Photographs, Whipple-Callender Architects, Portland, ME; (right) Photo © Robert Perron, Photographer, Eastern Timber Homes, Leverett, NH.

p. 93: (top) Photo © Jessie Walker; (bottom) Photo © Brian Vanden Brink, Photographer 2003.

p. 94: (top) Photo © Jessie Walker; (bottom) Photo © Mark Samu, courtesy Hearst Specials.

p. 95: Photo by David Ericson, courtesy Fine Homebuilding, © The Taunton Press, Inc., Architect: Patrick McClane, Richmond, VA.

p. 96: (left) Photo © Robert Perron, Photographer, Landscape: Anne Penniman, Essex, CT; (top right) Photo © 2003 carolynbates.com, Artist: Don Kjelleren, Charlotte, VT; (bottom right) Photo © Brian Vanden Brink, Photographer 2003, Horiuchi & Solien Landscape Architects, Falmouth, MA.

p. 97: Photo © Robert Perron, Photographer, Architect: Paul Bailey, New Haven, CT.

p. 98: (top left) Photo © Brian Vanden Brink, Photographer 2003, Centerbrook Architects, Essex, CT; (bottom left) Photo © Robert Perron, Photographer; (right) Photo © Mark Samu, Architect: Mojo Stumer AIA, Roslyn, NY.

p. 99: Photo © Robert Perron, Photographer, Landscape: Anne Penniman, Essex, CT.

p. 100: (top) Photo © Brian Vanden Brink, Photographer 2003, Architect: Roc Caivano, Bar Harbor, ME; (bottom) Photo © Robert Perron, Photographer, Landscape: Shep Butler, Thetford, VT.

p. 101: (top) Photo © davidduncanlivingston.com; (bottom) Photo © davidduncanlivingston.com.

p. 102: Photo © 2003 carolynbates.com, General contractor: Tom Clark, A. W. Clark Jr. & Son, Inc., Waitsfield, VT.

p. 103: (left) Photo © Steven House, Architect: House + House, San Francisco, CA; (top right) Photo © Robert Perron, Photographer, Architect: Don Watson, Troy, NY; (bottom right) Photo © Robert Perron, Photographer, Architect: Don Watson, Troy, NY.

p. 104: (top) Photo © Robert Perron, Photographer, Builder: Steve Cavanaugh, Hamden, CT; (bottom) Photo © Robert Perron, Photographer.

p. 105: (top) Photo © davidduncanlivingston.com; (bottom) Photo © Robert Perron, Photographer, Architect: Gisolfi Associates, Hastings on Hudson, NY.

p. 106: (top) Photo © 2003 carolynbates.com, General contractor: Tom Sheppard, Sheppard Custom Homes, Inc., Williston, VT; (bottom) Photo © davidduncanlivingston.com.

p. 107: Photo © davidduncanlivingston.com.

p. 108: Photo © Mark Samu, Architect: Mojo Stumer, AIA, Roslyn, NY.

p. 109: (top) Photo © davidduncanlivingston.com; (bottom) Photo © Mark Samu, Architect: Noelker & Hull Associates, Chambersburg, PA.

p. 110: (top) Photo © davidduncanlivingston.com; (bottom left) Photo © Robert Perron, Photographer, Landscape: Janet Cavanaugh, VT; (bottom right) Photo © davidduncanlivingston.com.

p. 111: Photo © Robert Perron, Photographer, Designer: Leslie Darroch, Branford, CT.

p. 112: Photo © Brian Vanden Brink, Photographer 2003, Horiuchi & Solien Landscape Architects, Falmouth, MA.

p. 113: (left) Photo © Robert Perron, Photogra-

pher, Landscape: Rob Besser, New York, NY; (right) Photo © 2003 carolynbates.com, Architect: Frederick Horton, FW Horton & Associates, Shelburne, VT.

p. 114: (top) Photo © 2003 carolynbates.com, Cushman & Beckstrom Architecture and Planning, Inc., Stowe, VT; (bottom) Photo © Jessie Walker.

p. 115: Photo © Brian Vanden Brink, Photographer 2003, Weatherend Estate Furniture, Rockland, ME.

p. 116 (top) Photo © 2003 carolynbates.com, Architect: Dick Robson, Robson Bilgen Architects, Hancock, VT; (bottom) Photo © Brian Vanden Brink, Photographer 2003, Horiuchi & Solien Landscape Architects, Falmouth, MA.

p. 117: (top) Photo © 2003 carolynbates.com, Design: Darryl and Carol Davis, Davis Creative Building & Design, Barton, VT; (bottom) Photo © davidduncanlivingston.com.

p. 118: (top) Photo © Brian Vanden Brink, Photographer 2003, Centerbrook Architects, Essex, CT; (bottom) Photo © 2003 carolynbates.com, General contractor: Tom Sheppard, Sheppard Custom Homes, Inc., Williston, VT, Designer: Donna W. Sheppard, Williston, VT.

p. 119: Photo © Brian Vanden Brink, Photographer 2003, Weston & Hewitson Architects, Hingham, MA.

p. 120: (left) Photo © 2003 carolynbates.com, David Sellers, Sellers and Company, Architects, Warren, VT, General contractor: Rick Moore Construction, Killington, VT; (right) Photo © Brian Vanden Brink, Photographer 2003, Architect: Dominic Mercadante, Belfast, ME.

p. 121: (top) Photo © Brian Vanden Brink, Photographer 2003, Mark Hutker & Associates, Architects, Vineyard Haven, MA.

p. 122: (left) Photo © Mark Samu, Design: Lucianna Samu, Saratoga Springs, NY; (right) Photo © Robert Perron, Photographer.

p. 123: (left) Photo © davidduncanlivingston.com; (right) Photo © Robert Perron, Photographer.

p. 124: (top) Photo © Brian Vanden Brink, Photographer 2003, Mark Hutker & Associates, Architects, Vineyard Haven, MA; (bottom) Photo © Mark Samu, courtesy Hearst Specials.

p. 125: (left) Photo © Robert Perron, Photographer; (right) Photo © Brian Vanden Brink, Photographer 2003.

p. 126: Photo © Brian Vanden Brink, Photographer 2003, Weston & Hewitson Architects, Hingham, MA.

p. 127: (left) Photo © Brian Vanden Brink, Photographer 2003, Architect: Scott Simons, Yarmouth, ME; (right) Photo © Jessie Walker.

p. 128: (left) Photo © Jessie Walker; (right) Photo © Brian Vanden Brink, Photographer 2003, Horiuchi & Solien Landscape Architects, Falmouth, MA.

p. 129: (top) Photo © 2003 carolynbates.com, Office of H. Keith Wagner, Landscape Architects, Burlington, VT; (bottom) Photo © Robert Perron, Photographer.

p. 130: (top) Photo © Brian Vanden Brink, Photographer 2003, Architect: Peter Eisenman, New York, NY; (bottom) Photo © Robert Perron, Photographer, Landscape: Doug MacClise.

p. 131: Photos © 2003 carolynbates.com, Ted Montgomery, Project Architect, Indiana Architecture & Design, Charlotte, VT.

p. 132: (left) Photo by Scott Gibson, courtesy Fine Homebuilding, © The Taunton Press, Inc., Architect: Michael McKinley, Stonington, CT; (right) Photo © Brian Vanden Brink, Photographer 2003.

p. 133: Photo © Robert Perron, Photographer, Design: Gisolfi Associates, Hastings on Hudson, NY.

p. 134: (top) Photo © Ken Gutmaker; (bottom) Photo © Brian Vanden Brink, Photographer 2003, Horiuchi & Solien Landscape Architects, Falmouth, MA.

p. 135: (top) Photo by Charles Miller, courtesy Fine Homebuilding, © The Taunton Press, Inc.; architect: Jan Wisniewski, Santa Fe, NM; (bottom) Photo © Robert Perron, Photographer, Landscape: Doug Kycia, Bethany, CT.

p. 136: (left) Photo © Brian Vanden Brink, Photographer 2003, Architect: Jack Silverio, Lincolnville, ME; (right) Photo © Brian Vanden Brink, Photographer 2003, Mark Hutker & Associates, Architects, Vineyard Haven, MA.

p. 137: (top) Photo © Brian Vanden Brink, Photographer 2003; (bottom) Photo © Brian Vanden Brink, Photographer 2003, Design: Io Oaks, IOI Inc., Boston, MA.

p. 138: Photo © Robert Perron, Photographer, Architect: Marvin Michaelson, Hamden, CT.

p. 139: (top) Photo © davidduncanlivingston.com; (bottom) Photo © Brian Vanden Brink, Photographer 2003, Weatherend Estate Furniture, Rockland, ME.

p. 140: (top) Photo © Brian Vanden Brink, Photographer 2003, Architect: Steven Foote, Boston, MA; (bottom) Photo © Brian Vanden Brink, Photographer 2003, Architect: Steven Foote, Boston, MA.

p. 141: (top) Photo © Robert Perron, Photographer, Builder: Steve Cavanaugh, Hamden, CT; (bottom) Photo © Robert Perron, Photographer, Landscape: Shep Butler, Thetford, VT.

p. 142: (left) Photo © Robert Perron, Photographer, Architect: Chris Woerner, Stylist: Pam Moriarty, Branford, CT; (top right) Photo © Brian Vanden Brink, Photographer 2003, Design: Axel Berg, Inc., Falmouth, ME; (bottom right) Photo © Mark Samu, Design: Lucianna Samu, Saratoga Springs, NY.

p. 143: (top) Photo © Brian Vanden Brink, Photographer 2003, Horiuchi & Solien Landscape Architects, Falmouth, ME; (bottom) Photo © Robert Perron, Photographer, Landscape: Doug MacClise.

p. 144: Photo © Brian Vanden Brink, Photographer 2003, Mark Hutker & Associates, Architects, Vineyard Haven, MA.

p. 145: (top) Photo © Robert Perron, Photographer; architect: Paul Bailey, New Haven, CT; (bottom) Photo © davidduncanlivingston.com.

p. 146: (left) Photo © Jessie Walker; (right) Photo © 2003 carolynbates.com, David Sellers, Sellers and Co. Architects, Warren, VT.

p. 147: (top) Photo © Brian Vanden Brink, Photographer 2003, Architect: Scott Simons, Portland, ME; (bottom) Photo © Mark Samu; courtesy Hearst Specials.

p. 148: (top) Photo © davidduncanlivingston.com; (bottom) Photo © Jessie Walker.

p. 149: (top) Photo by Kim Brun, courtesy California Redwood Association, Design: L. Dennis Shields, Laguna Hills, CA.; (bottom) Photo © davidduncanlivingston.com.

p. 150: (top) Photo © davidduncanlivingston.com; (bottom) Photo © Brian Vanden Brink, Photographer 2003.

p. 151: (top left)Photo © davidduncanlivingston.com; (top right) Photo © Brian Vanden Brink, Photographer 2003, Architect: Alan Freysinger, Milwaukee, WI; (bottom) Photo © Robert Perron, Photographer, Architect: Paul Bailey, New Haven, CT.

p. 152: (left) Photo © davidduncanlivingston.com; (top right) Photo © Brian Vanden Brink, Photographer 2003, Weatherend Estate Furniture, Rockland, ME; (bottom right) Photo © davidduncanlivingston.com.

p. 153: (top) Photo © davidduncanlivingston.com; (bottom) Photo © davidduncanlivingston.com.

CHAPTER 4

p. 154: Photo © davidduncanlivingston.com.

p. 155: Photo © Brian Vanden Brink, Photographer 2003.

p. 156: (top) Photo © Robert Perron, Photographer, Designer: Leslie Darroch, Branford, CT; (bottom) Photo © 2003 carolynbates.com, Architect: Malcolm Appleton, AIA, Waitsfield, VT.

p. 157: Photos © Robert Perron, Photographer, 2003.

p. 158: Photo © Robert Perron, Photographer, Landscape: Shep Butler, Thetford, VT.

p. 159: (top right) Photo © Mark Samu, Design: Lucianna Samu, Saratoga Springs, NY; (top right) Photo © Robert Perron, Photographer; (bottom) Photo © Brian Vanden Brink, Photographer 2003, Mark Hutker & Associates, Architects, Vineyard Haven, MA.

p. 160: Photo © Mark Samu, courtesy Hearst Specials.

p. 161: (left) Photo © Jessie Walke; (right) Photo © Brian Vanden Brink, Photographer 2003, Architect: Stephen Foote, Boston, MA.

p. 162: (left)Photo © Brian Vanden Brink, Photographer 2003, Ron Forest Fences, Scarborough, ME; (right) Photo © Robert Perron, Photographer, Architect: Nelson Denny, Hadlyme, CT.

p. 163: (left) Photo © Jessie Walker; (right) Photo © 2003 carolynbates.com, Builder: Tom Sheppard, Sheppard Custom Homes, Inc., Williston, VT.

p. 164: (top) Photo © Robert Perron, Photographer, Landscaper: Doug Kycia, Bethany, CT; (bottom) Photo © Brian Vanden Brink, Photographer 2003, Ron Forest Fences, Scarborough, ME.

p. 165: Photos © 2003 carolynbates.com, Cushman & Beckstrom Architecture and Planning, Inc., Stowe, VT.

p. 166: (top) Photo © davidduncanlivingston.com; (bottom) Photo © 2003 carolynbates.com, Office of H. Keith Wagner, Landscape Architects, Burlington, VT.

p. 167: (top) Photos © Robert Perron, Photographer, Architect: Melanie Taylor, New Haven, CT; (bottom) Photo © Brian Vanden Brink, Photographer, 2003; Horiuchi & Solien Landscape Architects, Falmouth, MA.

p. 168: Photos © Brian Vanden Brink, Photographer, 2003; Sam Williamson, Landscape Architect, Portland, OR.

p. 169: (top) Photo © Brian Vanden Brink, Horiuchi & Solien Landscape Architects, Falmouth, MA, Artist: Charles Swanson, South Dartmouth, MA; (bottom) Photo © Brian Vanden Brink, Ron Forest Fences, Scarborough, ME.